Sefer Ha-Goralot
The Book of Oracles

Sefer Ha-Goralot
The Book of Oracles

By Rabbi Chaim Vital

Translated by Elyakim Getz

E-mail: info@everburninglight.org
WWW: http://www.everburninglight.org

Publisher: Providence University
First edition, 2007
ISBN: 1-897352-16-6

Copyright © 2007 by Fabrizio Lanza, ULC-ITALIA
For information:
ULC-ITALIA
Via C.A. Colombo 20/F, 34074 Monfalcone (GO)
Tel.: +39-(0)481-412574

Index of contents

Preface

This book of Rabbi Chaim Vital contains two-hundred-fifty-six questions according to the Zodiac and the seven planets. It includes the names of the angels who are appointed to these planets and the twelve constellations. It tells which prayers to say before the casting of the lot, as well as which day and hour to ask.

Among these questions, one may ask about his own reincarnation, and which commandment (*Mitzva*) he has come to repair in this world.

Many questions may be asked about all aspects of life: marriage, children, health, business, theft, and even the days of the Messiah.

The transliteration of Hebrew characters follows the usual way of English translation, except for the following ones:

Heth = 'h

Teth = t

Kuf = q

Ayin = '(plus the relevant letter)

Shin = sh

A special thanks to Talib Din for his support in editing and proofreading the translation.

Elyakim Getz

[1] Introduction of the Author, Rabbi Chaim Vital

Let the intelligent begin and the lot be cast (יַפְתַּח הַמַשְׂכִּיל וַיַפִיל פּוּר הוּא) [in this sentence, the name IHVH is spelled]. I cannot speak in a grandiose manner, for I saw the evil of our people. I also heard that many are not careful and ask necromancers or spirits about theft or other matters, and thus enjoy sorcery. Therefore, I wrote this booklet and revealed a mystery, even if it is improper. I did so that they should know that there is a God and there are prophets in Israel, and that no one should seek sorcery.

Before anything, I shall write the seven planets ruling the days of the week followed by the twelve constellations:

Sunday: The sun rules during the first hour, while the other hours [and planets] follow accordingly.

Monday: The moon rules during the first hour.

Tuesday: Mars rules during the first hour.

Wednesday: Mercury rules during the first hour.

Thursday: Jupiter rules during the first hour.

Friday: Venus rules during the first hour.

Sabbath: Saturn rules during the first hour.

These are the mnemonic signs for the hours of the days and the nights: for the beginnings of the days, *Chl"m Ktzn"sh* (חל"ם כצנ"ש) (*Chamah-Levanah-Ma'adim, Kokhav-Tzedeq-Nogah-Shabtay*). For the beginnings of the night: *Ktzn"sh Chl"m* (כצנ"ש חל"ם).

These are the angels ruling over the seven planets: *Kaftzie"l* (קפציאל) rules over Saturn, *Tzadkie"l* (צדקיאל) over Jupiter, *Samae"l* (סמאל) over Mars, *Rafae"l* (רפאל) over the Sun, *'Anae"l* (ענאל) over Venus, *Mikhae"l* (מיכאל) over Mercury, and *Gavrie"l* (גבריאל) over the Moon.

These are the angels ruling over the twelve constellations: *Chasdie"l* (חסדיאל) rules over Aries, *Barqie"l* (ברקיאל) over

Taurus, *Nurie"l* (נוריאל) over Gemini, *Ra'amie"l* (רעמיאל) over Cancer, *Sarvie"l* (סרביאל) (or *Sridie"l*, שרידיאל) over Leo, *Sririe"l* (סריריאל) (or *Adirie"l* – אדיריאל – and [2] *Sridie"l* – שרידיאל) over Virgo, *Ananie"l* (עניניאל) over Libra, *Lahaqie"l* (להקיאל) over Scorpio, *Tzadqie"l* (צדקיאל) (or *Nehaqie"l*, נהקיאל) over Saggitarius, *Qabnie"l* (קבניאל) over Capricornus, *Qanae"l* (קנאל) over Aquarius, and *Sraharie"l* (סרהריאל) (or *Soharie"l*, סוהריאל) over Pisces.

You must know that every day is named after the planet that rules during its first hour. Therefore, do not cast the lot on the holy *Sabbath* ruled by Saturn, not on Tuesday ruled by Mars, and not on Wednesday ruled by Mercury, except for three things: Saturn for a treasure, Mars for war and money, and Mercury for wisdom and writing. So, you shall cast the lot only on Sunday, Monday, Thursday, and Friday. But even on these days, do not cast the lot in the hours ruled by Saturn, Mars, and Mercury. Likewise, do not cast the lot on a cloudy day, and not on the day preceding the new moon, not on the new moon itself, and not on the following day. When you cast the lot, make sure you determine the hour of the day, the ministering planet, and its ruling angel. Then, adjure them and call them, so that they direct your hand to a good, right, and true place. This way, the answer to your question will be truthful and in accordance with the lot.

Know that, when you open the book, you have to count seven times seven. Look in the book of answers, and see in which section the letter corresponding to the letter of your lot has been laid. There is your answer.

This prayer is to be said seven times before the casting of the lot

"Please, with the might of your right untie the knot (*Ana be-Koach Gedulath Yeminkhah Tatir Tzerurah*)". When saying this prayer, have in mind that your book should bring a solution and that your question should be answered. Then say once: "Accept our plea and hear our cry, He Who knows hidden things (*Shav'atenu Qabel u-Shm'a Tza'aqatenu Yode'a Ta'alumoth*)". Have in mind that your prayer should be answered and the secret of your answer should be revealed. Think also that [in that prayer] there are forty-nine words and seven verses corresponding to the casting of the lots. Then say: "May it be Your will, O Eternal, the God of our forefathers, the God of Abraham, the God of Isaac, the God of Jacob, the God of Moses, the God of Aaron, the God of Pinchas, the God of David. Act for the sake of the merit of these seven righteous ones, for the sake of Your seven emanations: Benevolence, Severity, Beauty, Victory, Glory, Foundation, and Kingdom, which lead all [3] the worlds. Lead me, and guide me on the right path, and let me know the truthful answer to my question that is so and so (here one must detail the question with a perfect heart, firm knowledge, and without any confusion. It would be all the better to cast the lot in a special place, in total privacy, in order not to be disturbed). May the book open up in a right and true place, in a way that it will bring up the fiftieth letter as the letter of truth. Let it be the right answer according to the order of this holy lottery. Act for the sake of Your seven emanations, which, from seven to seven, reach forty-nine; for the sake of the psalm I recited in front of You and that has seven verses and forty-nine words; for the sake of the fifty gates of Understanding, which are the living God (*Elohim Chaim*); for the sake of the seven books; for the sake of the seven holy temples; for the sake of the seven heavens, the seven planets, the seven angels who minister the King, the Eternal of the armies. After the seven mentioned ways, let me know the true answer to my question, without any doubt. You desired and chose these lots, as it is written in your *Torah* (Numbers 26:55): 'The land shall be divided by lots'. And so it was with lots that you separated between the goat for the

Eternal and the goat for 'Azazel. Therefore, may it be Your Will, O Eternal, the God of our forefathers, to let me know the true answer to my question through this lot, without any doubt; for the sake of your name, which comes out of the end letters of the verse (Leviticus 16:8), 'And Aaron shall cast lots upon the two goats; one for the Eternal, and the other for 'Azazel [*ve-Natan Aharon 'al Shnei ha-S'eirim Goraloth, Goral Echad la-Yhvh ve-Goral Echad la-'Azazel*]', and this is the humble persistent gate (לְדַלָּה דְלָתַם יְלָנָן). May the star so and so be upon you with the prince so and so, on such and such hour. May it be with the power of the angel so and so, which is appointed upon you; by the name of He Who created you in heaven, by the power of the higher Understanding. Help me right with this lottery, and guide my hand to open the book truly and rightfully. Let it fall upon the fiftieth letter, and the answer to my question will be true, without any doubt, and according to the order written in this holy lottery".

Then, say the Psalm *Mikhtam le-David* once; then, seven times the verse (Deuteronomy 33:4), "Moses commanded us a *Torah*, the inheritance of the congregation of Jacob", which has seven words: seven times seven words, amounting to forty-nine words.

Then, say the verse (Psalm 16:5) seven times, "The Eternal is the portion of my inheritance". Have in mind that this verse has seven words and that seven times amounts to forty-nine. Then, open the book between your two hands and do this: start to count from the beginning of that page until you reach the fiftieth letter: there is your answer.

[4] This is the prayer for knowing the mystery of reincarnation (*Gilgul*)

May it be Your Will, O Eternal, crowned God, Magnificent, Glorified, steadfast in your thirteen attributes – (Exodus 34:6-7), "Eternal, Eternal (1) mighty, (2) merciful, (3) gracious, (4-5) slow to anger (*Erekh Apayim*), (6) abundant in love, (7) and truth, (8) extending kindness, (9) to thousands, (10) forgiving iniquity, (11) and transgression, (12) and sin; (13) yet He does not remit all punishment" – who shows mercy to thousands of generations of those who love Him, to those who keep His precepts, and act with love and compassion with them. He produces the causes and revolves the migration of souls, so that none should be outcast. You desire the welfare of the wicked, as you said through your prophet (Ezekiel 18:23), "Have I any pleasure at all that the wicked should die? – says the Eternal God: and not that he should return from his ways and live?". And it is said (Ezekiel 33:11), "Turn, turn from your evil ways: for why will you die, O house of Israel?". And again (Hoshea 14:3), "Take with you words and turn to the Eternal". Therefore, I took it to heart to return to You in perfect repentance and to knock on Your door. Relying on Your great love, I came with Your thirteen attributes, which do not come back empty from Your presence. I trust in their merit, as you said in your *Torah* (Exodus 20:6), "But I show mercy to thousands of generations", for You show mercy to Your creatures, even for thousands of generations, until they are corrected, so that they should not perish. So I came knocking on Your door, in order to implore favor by the merit of Your *Torah* and of your thirteen attributes, which do not come back empty from Your presence. It is written about them (Exodus 34:7), "Extending kindness to thousands" – Keep Your kindness with me: reward me with grace and benevolence, and let me know the root of my *Neshamah* (נשמה, [higher] Soul) through this lottery: what is its task and how does one correct it? I took it to heart to return to You in perfect repentance, and I come now to You with a broken and crushed heart: my God do not despise me! I am asking of You to let me know my shortcomings and lackings, and how to correct them. Do not let any sin or transgression hold back my prayer! Delve under the throne of Your glory and stretch Your arm under the wings of the *Keruvim* (כרובים), in order to receive my prayer and supplication. Send the angel appointed over the lots to prevent my hand from erring, and direct it to the place of truth and uprightness. When I shall open the book, let the fiftieth letter provide the right answer, clear of any stumbling-block; a true answer that tells me the root of my *Neshamah*: its blemish and [5] its lacking. My transgressions are great; like a heavy load, they weigh on me. I cannot open my mouth to speak or raise my forehead. Everyday I say, "I shall sin and then repent", but I am unable to return. I dread to be pushed away by the bright blade of the revolving sword that keeps the way to the Garden of Eden. Therefore, I rely on your thirteen attributes: Eternal, Eternal, mighty, merciful, gracious, slow to anger, abundant in love, in truth, extending kindness to thousands, forgiving iniquity and transgression, and sin; yet He does not remit all punishment. Submit all judgements by their merit, and for their sake let my prayer come before You: for the sake of your higher Crown, and for the sake of its thirteen virtues; for the sake of the name *Ehye"h* (אהי"ה) alluded to in it; for the sake of your mysterious Wisdom, and for the sake of the thirty-two ways spreading from it; for the sake of your name *Y"H* (י"ה) alluded to in it; for the sake of Your hidden Understanding, and for the sake of the fifty gates of Understanding that are opened in it; for the sake of Your name *Yèhovih* (יְהֹוִה) alluded to in it; for the sake of the proper Knowledge with which abysses, valleys and chambers are to be filled; for the sake of the name *Yohêvahê* (יֹהֶוָהֶ), which is alluded to in it; for the sake of your higher Benevolence, through which You give benevolence to all; for the sake of the seventy-two names derived from the three verses (Exodus 14:19), "And he went [*Va-Yis"'a*]", (Exodus 14:20) "And it came [*va-Yav"o*]", (Exodus 14:21) "And he stretched out [*va-Yêṭ*]", which allude to it; for the sake of Your Name alluded to in it; for the sake of your Severity, and for the sake of the forty-two heavenly essences (*Havayoth*) from the head and hand phylacteries; for the sake of the forty-two letters coming out of the *Beit* (house) of (Genesis 1:1), "In the beginning (*Bereshith*)", until the *Vav* of (Genesis 1:2) "And void (*va-Vohu*)", the letters with which the heavens and the earth were created; for the sake of the forty-two lettered Name coming out of the prayer

"Please, with the might (*Ana be-Koach*)", which is its sheath; for the sake of *Elohim* (אלהים) alluded to in it; for the sake of Your Beauty, a pleasant countenance; for the sake of the seventy faces spreading from it through the middle line; for the sake of *Yhv"h* (שם הויה) punctuated like *Tzevaoth* (צבאות), which is alluded to in it; for the sake of Your Victory, the Victory of Israel, which does not lie and does not deceive, the right column called *Yakhin* (יכין); for the sake of the Name, the God of the armies (*Tzevaoth*) alluded to in it; for the sake of Your Glory and majesty, where You dress in glory and majesty, the left column called *Boaz* (בועז); for the sake of the name *Elohim Tzevaoth* (שם אלהים צבאות) alluded to in it; for the sake of your Foundation, the righteous foundation of the universe from Zion, the perfection of beauty; for the sake of the name *El Shaday* (אל שדי) alluded to in it; for the sake of Your Kingdom, the everlasting kingdom, the mistress of the home – Your Name alluded to in it is *Adonay* (אדני), for You are the Lord of all Worlds. With strength and power You bring back the *Neshamoth*; You accept the prayers, as it is written (Psalm 51:17), "O lord (*Adonay*), [6] open my lips, and my mouth shall declare Your praise". Open Your door and accept my prayer; listen to my cry; fulfill my request, as it is written (Psalm 145: 16), "You open your hand [*Poteach Eth Yadeikha*] and satisfy [*u-Masby'a*, it has the same numerical value as *Cht"kh*] the desire of every living thing". You should supply, bring forth, fulfill my will, and let me know the truth about this matter: what is the root of my *Neshamah*? Let me know its lacking and its blemish; send the angel appointed over the lots to direct my hand to the right and truthful place; bring about the answer with the letters, from one lot to another, as they are arranged in this book, with no mistake and no lie or deceit. Just like You are truthful, O Eternal, our God, so let me know truth and uprightness. Let me know how to come back to You in perfect repentance. Accept my prayer and my repentance. May my words and the meditation of my heart be acceptable to You, my Rock and Redeemer.

Then, one should say the prayer composed for the lottery, but instead of saying "my request is so and so", one should mention the subject of reincarnation, that he wants to know the root of his *Neshamah*. Likewise, he should mention the precepts he still needs to perform followed by his transgressions. After the prayer for the lottery, open the book.

Know that even if you need a hundred lots to know one name or anything else, everything will be seen at the first opening and with the completion of the fiftieth letter. The page in which the letter of the lot is found does not count, for it is within the boundary of the first lot. From the end of that page, start to count seven times seven, according to the known order. This is called the second lot, and the letter that comes up after the seven known ways is the letter of the second lot. Following this method, you will bring up a third and a fourth lot, and so on infinitely, according to your needs. So, you can go back to the end of the page in which the letter of the first lot was and start to count for the second lot. At the end of the page of the second lot, start to count for the third lot, etc., and so, as much as needed, from lot to lot, until your answer comes up. Understand this!

Prayer for finding a treasure

May it be your will, O Eternal, God of our forefathers, God of the armies; Who sits over the *Keruvim*, *El Shaday*, Who dispenses blessings without end; the Almighty, compassionate father, Who causes relief and shows favor; Who opens the gates and brings satisfaction to all requests; the Almighty, Who feeds the wild ox as well as the louse; the Almighty *Adonay*, the God of Israel, the shield of David, God of the Chariot; Who makes poor and makes rich, brings low and raises up; Who is full of goodness and brings forth the will of all who ask. Grant me my wish and let me know the place of a hidden treasure, so that your servant may live with a perfect heart and perform deeds of charity and benevolence with the poor; so that he may learn, teach and support *Torah* scholars, as it is known and revealed before the throne of your glory. Please, O God, God of my forefathers, I wish to perform deeds of charity with your creatures, to support *Torah* scholars and learn day and night. But our transgressions have increased, and the curtain between You and us has thickened; Your goodness has decreased, poverty prevails and prosperity has deserted Israel; my heart tells me to act, but I cannot undertake anything. Therefore, I took it to heart to knock on your door, on the gates of your compassion, in order to supplicate and pray before You: O God of Israel, do not send me empty handed from before You. For your sake and for the sake of Your holy and pure angels who are appointed over all treasures of the world, guide my hand to the right place. Let me open the book, and after seven time seven ways, at the fiftieth letter, may I find the right answer to my request, whether by strike or by number, so that I will not need to cast the lot again. But let me find the treasure with this lot. Let it be of a decent value, so that I can fulfill my desire to serve You without any doubt; without any kind of magic; without injury, neither physical nor spiritual. Rather, let it establish me in a place where I shall find gratification. Amen. May it be your will.

I adjure you Saturn and *Qaftzie"l* (קפצי"אל) the angel, by the name of the angel *Meṭaṭron* (מטטרון) who rules over you and whose name is as his Master's; by the power of the seventy names of *Metatron*, the chief of the service; by the power of the seventy thrones of the Master of [8] the world; by the power of the first name of the prayer "Please, with the might", *Ab"g yt"tz* (**אב״ג יח״ץ**), which rules over you; by the power of *Tsh"kh* (**תש״ך**) and by the transpositions of this name; by the power of *Adonay* (**אדני**) the God of Israel; by the power of the holy *Sabbath* and its mysteries; come and stand by my hand, over a good place; let me find the rightful and truthful answer. I adjure you by God, by the true God of Israel: establish me with truth, honor the God of Israel and His holy Names that I mentioned over you. Come down swiftly, and act according to my request: help me find the place of the treasure through this lot. Teach me truth and righteousness; act now. Come swiftly, and answer my request! Amen.

Then say the known prayer for the lottery, but instead of saying "my request is so and so", mention the treasure.

Prayer for knowing occult things, like the end of days, etc.

May it be Your will, O Eternal, God of our forefathers, the hidden Almighty Who hides in adornment where no heart or eye can reach Him; He who tells the end from the beginning; Who reveals the redemption of the remnant [of his people], the Will of all Wills (*Ra'ava de-R'auta*); Who reveals the depth and the hidden; Who knows the darkness and with whom the light resides; He Who reveals the depth from the darkness and foresees a thousand generations; the Almighty Who speaks and does; Who decrees and executes; You decreed this long and bitter exile on us, where all vision is closed and the end sealed; there is no rest, and the mysterious time has not yet arrived. All timings of redemption have ended and are no more; nothing is left but repentance, which comes at night and leaves in the morning. I know, O Eternal, God of our forefathers, that it is hidden and sealed from the eye of all seers. And who will come to the prophet and let him know the innermost thing? It is the heart who knows all mysteries (*Razin Stimin*). And whoever has a *Neshamah* within him hears the spirit (*Ruach*) of God speaking, but no one else knows of it, for the heart does not reveal anything to the mouth. And so, how do I dare to ask this from the Almighty, as I am only ash and a worm, and so *Masha"l* (מש"אל), *Eltzafa"n* (אלצ"פון), *and Sitr"i* (סת"רי). But I set my heart before Your everlasting compassion, O living God (*Elohim Chaim*) and King of the World (*Melekh 'Olam*), Who [9] is alluded to in the sabbatical year and in the great jubilee, in the refuge (*Ma'oz*) and in the tower (*Migdol*) of salvation; Who brings out of slavery to freedom, and in Whom the final redemption is revealed. Although, these are incomprehensible, I shall come with might, *Adonay Yhwh* (אדני יהוה), and call You in truth; answer me truthfully, as it is written (Psalm 145:18), "The Eternal is near to all those who call upon him, to all who call upon him in truth".

Then say nine times the verse (Psalm 119:145), "I cry with all my heart; answer me, O Eternal: I will keep your statutes", which correspond to the nine corrections (*Tiqunin*) of the Microprosopus (*Z'air Anpin*). When saying "with all", have in mind that it is an expression for the Gates of Understanding; and for the word "heart" (*Lev*), think of the thirty-two paths of Wisdom [*Lev* = *Lamed-Beit* = thirty-two]; and when saying "answer me, O Eternal", have in mind that He should answer you through the middle line (*Qav ha-Emts'ayi*), which is the name of *Havaya* (הויה), blessed be He.

May it be Your Will, O Eternal, God of our forefathers; for the sake of Your three Names that are written in Your Torah, *Ehye"h Asher Ehye"h* (אהי"ה אשר אהי"ה), which allude to the three hidden heads: Crown, Wisdom, Understanding; it is with three Names that You revealed the final redemption to Moses, our teacher, may he rest in peace; and now for the sake of these Names and for the sake of the seven corrections of the head of the Macroprosopus (*Arikh Anpin*), for the thirty-two paths of wondrous Wisdom, for the sake of the fifty gates of Understanding, the place of freedom and redemption, let the great trump blast and reveal to us the time of the last redemption; let the sound of that trump be channeled through the middle column to Kingdom of the Divine World, and from there to *Yah Akatriel Yhvh Tzevaoth* (יה אכתריאל יהוה), into the World of Creation; and from *Yah Akatriel Yhvh Tzevaoth* to *Meṭaṭron*, the chief of the service, to the World of Formation; and from *Meṭaṭron* to *Sandalfon* (סנדלפון), the chief of the *Ofanim* (אופנים), who ties crowns for his master; and from *Sandalfon* to the constellation of the day, which is so and so, and to its angel so and so; and from that constellation, to such and such planet that rules this hour, and to its angel so and so; and let the angel so and so, who rules this hour, come and place my hand in the truthful place in this book, so that I understand and know the truth about the final redemption through this lot, without any lie or deceit. Let my hand stand on the right place and let my answer be right and clear according to the order of this lot. As for you, *Meṭaṭron* and *Sandalfon Ma"'a B'a"b* (מא"ע בע"ב), the explicit names coming out of the three verses: (Exodus 14:10) "And he went (*Va-Yis"'a*)", (Exodus 14:20) "And it came (*va-Yav"o*)", (Exodus 14:21) "And he stretched out (*va-Yêṭ*)"; and by the power of *Hhv"y* (ההו"י), blessed be He Who garbs Himself in them and vivifies them, as it is written in the *Torah* (Exodus 23:21), "For My Name is in him"; may you be granted permission from the Master of the Universe, the God of Israel, to reveal this mystery [10] to your angel so and so, of such and such constellation; and the angel of that constellation will hand over the mystery to the angel of such and such a constellation. Let the angel of that constellation come and set my hand to open the book, so that I will count seven things, and the fiftieth letter will be the true letter of the lot, the answer to my request; and so, with the letter of the second lot that I will reach after counting seven times seven things; let the fiftieth letter be the right and true one. Let these two letters together be the number of the answers to my request; in truth and by the power of the God of truth, let me stand on the truth, without any doubt.

These are the questions

Aries

1.	Under which star should I build a house?	Saturn starts
2.	Should I marry now or not?	Saturn ends
3.	If I buy this thing, will its value increase?	Jupiter starts
4.	Will I come back in peace if I take this road?	Jupiter ends
5.	If I propose to this girl, will she agree or not?	Mars starts
6.	Will I succeed if I walk in front of the prince?	Mars ends
7.	Will the price of oil rise this year or not?	Sun starts
8.	Are there robbers on this road or not?	Sun ends
9.	What sin did this man commit?	Venus starts
10.	Will the king of France or Italy win?	Venus ends
11.	Should I live in this city or in another?	Mercury starts
12.	Should I have a friend or stay alone?	Mercury ends
13.	Which one among the girls should I take?	Moon starts
14.	Should I divorce my wife or not?	Moon ends
15.	Will I be able to keep this wealth?	Aquarius starts
16.	Will I take another wife if my spouse dies	Aquarius ends
17.	[11] Who killed so and so, from what illness did he die?	Saturn starts
18.	Will I have more sons and daughters?	Saturn ends
19.	What is so and so's illness?	Jupiter starts
20.	Will this boat go in peace?	Jupiter ends
21.	Is so and so cheating me?	Mars starts
22.	Will I win if I go to court?	Mars ends

23.	What will it be with fruit-trees this year?	Sun starts
24.	How many robbers are there on the way?	Sun ends
25.	Is this girl a virgin or not?	Venus starts
26.	Who will win between these two?	Venus ends
27.	Should I live in this house or not?	Mercury starts
28.	Is this company good for me?	Mercury ends
29.	Which one should I take as a son-in-law?	Moon starts
30.	Should I marry my brother's wife or not?	Moon ends
31.	Should I marry this widow?	Aquarius starts
32.	What is so and so's constellation?	Aquarius ends

Gemini

33.	Are my brothers all good?	Saturn stars
34.	From which country is my wife?	Saturn ends
35.	What spirit is hitting so and so; is it a demon?	Jupiter starts
36.	Will I suffer on this sea trip?	Jupiter ends
37.	Did this man steal from me?	Mars starts
38.	Will I succeed to do this thing?	Mars ends
39.	Will this year be good for seeds?	Sun starts
40.	Is so and so alive or dead?	Sun ends
41.	Did my husband commit adultery or not?	Venus starts
42.	[12] Will they choose a great scholar this year?	Venus ends
43.	Did I leave the lost object in such and such a place?	Mercury starts
44.	Are my friends faithful to me or not?	Mercury ends

45.	Is this bridegroom good for my daughter or not?	Moon starts
46.	Will the slave that ran away return?	Moon ends
47.	What will so and so think about me?	Aquarius starts
48.	Is this betrothal the right one?	Aquarius ends

The Substance of Heaven

49.	Should I take a different store?	Saturn starts
50.	How many years will I live?	Saturn ends
51.	Will this patient heal with this amulet?	Jupiter starts
52.	Are there pirates on this sea trip?	Jupiter ends
53.	Who stole from so and so?	Mars starts
54.	Will this persecutor catch me or not?	Mars ends
55.	Will the price of wheat drop this year or not?	Sun starts
56.	Was so and so killed or not?	Sun ends
57.	Does my husband desire any woman?	Venus starts
58.	Will the one who was arrested be freed right away?	Venus ends
59.	What is my planet?	Mercury starts
60.	Who among the colleagues stole this?	Mercury ends
61.	What will happen to my daughter with this bridegroom?	Moon starts
62.	Did the slave escape to such and such a place?	Moon ends
63.	Is this widow a killer [a woman who became a widow for the second or the third time is called a killer, *Qatlanith*] or her match has not arrived?	Aquarius starts

| 64. | Under which star should this betrothal be decided? | Aquarius ends |

Cancer

65.	Will I gain if I join this partnership?	Saturn starts
66.	[13] How many children will I have?	Saturn ends
67.	What is the reason for her children's death?	Jupiter starts
68.	Is this rumor true or false?	Jupiter ends
69.	Is the thief a man or a woman?	Mars starts
70.	Will they try to catch me if I escape?	Mars ends
71.	Will there be rain this year?	Sun starts
72.	Will we find the one that was killed?	Sun ends
73.	Did my wife commit adultery or not?	Venus starts
74.	Why does the prince want to catch me?	Venus ends
75.	Is the last Messiah already born or not?	Mercury starts
76.	Is that stolen object already sold or not?	Mercury ends
77.	Is this precious stone good?	Moon starts
78.	Did that slave escape or is he hiding?	Moon ends
79.	Should I decide on this betrothal or not?	Aquarius starts
80.	On what day should I decide on this betrothal?	Aquarius ends
81.	Which one among the slaves should I take?	Saturn starts
82.	Will the one who drowns in the sea be saved?	Saturn ends
83.	If I make a potion for fertility, will it work?	Jupiter starts
84.	Did such and such a boat already leave?	Jupiter ends
85.	From which nationality is the thief?	Mars starts

86.	Will this newborn live or not?	Mars ends
87.	Is this house a good investment?	Sun starts
88.	Which field among these should I buy?	Sun ends
89.	Does my wife desire any man?	Venus starts
90.	The prince wants to see me; should I hide?	Venus ends
91.	Is my wife in this country or not?	Mercury starts
92.	Where is the theft?	Mercury ends
93.	Which one among these houses is good for me?	Moon starts
94.	[14] Will fish be caught if I throw the net?	Moon ends
95.	Is this woman so and so's mate?	Aquarius starts
96.	On which day should I decide to join in?	Aquarius ends

Virgo

97.	What will this pregnant woman give birth to?	Saturn starts
98.	How will so and so die?	Saturn ends
99.	From which illness will he die?	Jupiter starts
100.	Is the dream I dreamed true?	Jupiter ends
101.	Will my dream come true soon?	Mars starts
102.	Is my dream literal or not?	Mars ends
103.	If I run for this office will I obtain it?	Sun starts
104.	Is this office good for the children or not?	Sun ends
105.	Will I obtain such and such thing?	Venus starts
106.	Should I do such and such a thing because I desire it?	Venus ends
107.	Will I be guaranteed on this boat?	Mercury starts

108.	Should I take this boat?	Mercury ends
109.	Should I go by sea or by land?	Moon starts
110.	What is my messenger doing?	Moon ends
111.	Is the vision of so and so holy?	Aquarius starts
112.	Which good star should I connect with?	Aquarius ends

The West

113.	Under which good star should I sit in the store?	Saturn starts
114.	Which day of the week should I enter the house?	Saturn ends
115.	Which day of the month should I enter the house?	Jupiter starts
116.	Under which star should I run away from the prince?	Jupiter ends
117.	In which city will I profit?	Mars starts
118.	[15] In which month should I make a friend?	Mars ends
119.	Who broke such and such a thing?	Sun starts
120.	Are these pangs of birth or not?	Sun ends
121.	Who is so and so the *Nefesh* of?	Venus starts
122.	Is my *Neshamah* a new one or not?	Venus ends
123.	How many precepts have I not yet done?	Mercury starts
124.	Which undone precept caused me to reincarnate?	Mercury ends
125.	Which sins caused my reincarnation?	Moon starts
126.	How many times did I reincarnate?	Moon ends
127.	To which tribe do I belong?	Aquarius starts

128. Is my mother dead or sick?   Aquarius ends

Libra

129. Did my daughter give birth or not?   Saturn starts

130. Will I inherit someone in the future?   Saturn ends

131. Which day of the week should I travel?   Jupiter starts

132. What good day should I befriend this one?   Jupiter ends

133. Is this man lucky to do business with?   Mars starts

134. Which one among the stars is his constellation?   Mars ends

135. Does my son have boys or girls?   Sun starts

136. Is this medicine good for this illness?   Sun ends

137. Why is this girl's betrothal being delayed?   Venus starts

138. Which sin is causing my illness?   Venus ends

139. Which day of the month is propitious for action?   Mercury starts

140. Will I profit from this merchandise?   Mercury ends

141. Is this house good for the boys?   Moon starts

142. Was this thing lost or not?   Moon ends

143. Will my request from the demon be done or not?   Aquarius starts

144. Is so and so the thief or someone else?   Aquarius ends

145. [16] In which direction should I go to succeed?   Saturn starts

146. Will this new prince be good to us?   Saturn ends

147. What did my *Neshamah* come to learn?   Jupiter starts

148. Is this wife good for wealth or for children?   Jupiter ends

149.	Is my father dead or alive?	Mars starts
150.	Is the barrenness from her or from me?	Mars ends
151.	Which month was the theft performed?	Sun starts
152.	Is this merchandise stolen and should I buy it?	Sun ends
153.	Is there a lost object in this house?	Venus starts
154.	Where is the lost object located in the house?	Venus ends
155.	Where is the treasure hidden in the house?	Mercury starts
156.	Is the treasure buried deeply or not?	Mercury ends
157.	Is the treasure bewitched or not?	Moon starts
158.	Should I play dice or not?	Moon ends
159.	Was so and so negligent with the deposit?	Aquarius starts
160.	Should I learn such and such a trade?	Aquarius ends

Archer

161.	Was so and so released or not?	Saturn starts
162.	What does the thief look like?	Saturn ends
163.	Should I undertake this mission?	Jupiter starts
164.	Will the rule of this princess last?	Jupiter ends
165.	Should I learn *Kabbalah*, is there a liability?	Mars starts
166.	How many days should I stay on the sea?	Mars ends
167.	Is this woman my mate?	Sun starts
168.	Will this theft be found?	Sun ends
169.	If I send for a cure will it succeed?	Venus starts
170.	[17] Are my brothers good?	Venus ends

171.	Will I profit with this trade?	Mercury starts
172.	Is this suspicion about him true or not?	Mercury ends
173.	Will I come back in peace if I undertake this mission?	Moon starts
174.	Is the viceroy dead or was he put down?	Moon ends
175.	Why does so and so hate my wife?	Aquarius starts
176.	Is this woman pregnant or not?	Aquarius ends

The Substance of Earth

177.	Will this pregnant woman be saved?	Saturn starts
178.	Will my father come speedily or not?	Saturn ends
179.	Why did this betrothal not come through?	Jupiter starts
180.	Did so and so leave or not?	Jupiter ends
181.	If I ask the theft from the thief, will he give it to me?	Mars starts
182.	Will it be known if I start to look for the treasure?	Mars ends
183.	Which day is good to pulverize corn grains?	Sun starts
184.	Do my brothers have any children?	Sun ends
185.	Which trade will earn me more?	Venus starts
186.	Should I buy this animal?	Venus ends
187.	Is the suspect standing here?	Mercury starts
188.	Is the messenger alive, dead or sick?	Mercury ends
189.	Is it true that this woman is suspect of adultery?	Moon starts
190.	Why does this woman hate her husband?	Moon ends

191.	Will this patient heal from his illness?	Aquarius starts
192.	Is this baby born under a good star?	Aquarius ends

Capricorn

193.	Is my son living and healthy?	Saturn starts
194.	Should I travel alone?	Saturn ends
195.	Does so and so intend to return to his house?	Jupiter starts
196.	Will the lost object be found or not?	Jupiter ends
197.	Will I profit if I keep this merchandise?	Mars starts
198.	Will I succeed in the endeavor I intend to do?	Mars ends
199.	When is it appropriate to throw the cure?	Sun starts
200.	Will my brother have boys or girls?	Sun ends
201.	Should I rent this house?	Venus starts
202.	Will I profit if I buy this field?	Venus ends
203.	Is the coming messenger near or far?	Mercury starts
204.	Why does so and so hate so and so?	Mercury ends
205.	Is my family all good?	Moon starts
206.	How long will the newborn boy live?	Moon ends
207.	Does so and so love me the same as I love him?	Aquarius starts
208.	Who found this lost object?	Aquarius ends

Aquarius

209.	Will the vine give fruit, and what about the wine?	Saturn starts

210. Is it good for me to learn such and such wisdom?   Saturn ends

211. Which day of the month is good to pulverize corn?   Jupiter starts

212. Will he who goes out to war win?   Jupiter ends

213. Should I move my dwelling from this city?   Mars starts

214. Is it good for me to buy that slave?   Mars ends

215. How many thieves stole this thing?   Sun starts

216. Will this sorrow of mine last?   Sun ends

217. Will I attain my desire if I remain solitary?   Venus starts

218. Which day of the week is propitious to leave the city?   Venus ends

219. Will this newborn be wise or rich?   Mercury starts

220. To which religion belongs the one who hit so and so?   Mercury ends

221. [19] Will I profit this way?   Moon starts

222. Does this woman love me?   Moon ends

223. How many letters are there in the thief's name?   Aquarius starts

224. Are there pirates in such and such a place?   Aquarius ends

Pisces

225. Which sort of pirates are there in that place at sea?   Saturn starts

226. Who will win, Rome or Ismael?   Saturn ends

227. Is this store good for me?   Jupiter starts

228. Is it good to acquire this maidservant?   Jupiter ends

229. At what time was this object stolen?   Mars starts

230.	Does this messenger intend to return?	Mars ends
231.	How many illnesses will I suffer in my lifetime?	Sun starts
232.	Did so and so transgress with the deposit?	Sun ends
233.	Will the one who owes me deny it in court?	Venus starts
234.	Which day of the week should I sit in the store?	Venus ends
235.	Which day of the month should I sit in the store?	Mercury starts
236.	Under which good star should I enter this house?	Mercury ends
237.	Which day of the week is good to enter this place?	Moon starts
238.	Which day of the month should I enter the city?	Moon ends
239.	Which country is propitious for profit?	Aquarius starts
240.	Did so and so speak the truth or is he trying me?	Aquarius ends

East

241.	Will this woman miscarry?	Saturn starts
242.	What did my daughter in law give birth to?	Saturn ends
243.	Is my wife healthy and did she give birth?	Jupiter starts
244.	Will I find money in my lifetime?	Jupiter ends
245.	[20] Was my prayer accepted and my plea accomplished?	Mars starts
246.	Will I go out of this boat?	Mars ends
247.	Who will die first between these two?	Sun Starts

248. Are my deeds acceptable before the   Sun ends
     Omnipresent?

249. Will this messenger succeed by the prince Venus starts
     or not?

250. Up to what place does my place reach?   Venus ends

251. Which worlds were united through me?   Mercury starts

252. How many letters are there in the name of Mercury ends
     the Messiah?

253. How long ago was the Messiah, the son of   Moon starts
     David, born?

254. Will the redemption of Israel take place in Moon ends
     my lifetime?

255. Where in the world is the Messiah   Aquarius starts
     standing?

256. Which year will the redemption of Israel   Aquarius ends
     be?

This is the end of the questions. From here on, I shall write the questions and the answers together.

Behold, I must explain that whoever wants to know the answer to his question shall take the second part of the twenty-four books, i.e. Isaiah and Jeremiah, and divide each page in two. When you open the book, count seven pages and again seven pages, i.e. seven pages, as each one is divided in two. Then, count seven half pages, that is every page being two, and then seven verses, then seven lines, then seven words, then seven letters, and then see the eighth letter that is the fiftieth item of this count. Take this letter to the board of answers, and where you find this letter, there is your answer. This is enough for the one who understands.

These are the answers of the lottery

1

If you want to know under which good star you should build your house, organize the twelve constellations before you: Aries, Taurus, Gemini, Cancer, Lion, Virgo, Libra, [21] Scorpio, Sagittarius, Capricorn, Aquarius, and Pisces, and throw the lot. Count seven, as mentioned, and take the fiftieth letter. Then, take the second lot, as mentioned in the introduction. Count again seven times seven, take the fiftieth letter, and put it together with the first one. For instance, if the first letter was *Yod* and the second *Kaf*, say that ten times *Kaf* is two-hundred. Divide two-hundred by the twelve constellations, and whatever star comes last is the one for you to build your house under. You must start with Aries and finish with Pisces.

2

Take a wife, for it is good for you.	*Adzym 'aqtn* (אדזימעקתן)
Do not take a wife yet; wait a bit longer.	*Bh'hknprkp* (בההכנפרדף)
Do not take a wife in this town.	*Gvtlstzshtz* (גוטלסצששץ)

3

Buy this item, which will rise a lot.	*Avk'ashp* (אוכעשף)
This item will only rise a little.	*Bzlpttz* (בזלפתץ)
This one will neither rise nor drop.	*G'hmtzk* (גחמצך)
Do not take this one, for it will drop a little.	*Dtnqs* (דטנקס)

Do not take this one, for it will drop a lot.   *Hysrn* (היסרן)

4

Do not fear; you will return in peace.   *Azmqn* (אזמקן)

You will return in peace, but you will suffer and be saved.   *B'hnrp* (בחנרף)

You will suffer; they will dispossess you, but you will be saved.   *Gṯsshtz* (גטסשץ)

You will return in peace, but very sick, and you will be saved.   *Dy'at* (דיעת)

Accept God's decree, for this is the land where you'll die.   *Hkpk* (הכפך)

Beware not to go that way, for you won't return but be killed.   *Vltzm* (ולצם)

[22]

5

If you propose to the girl, she will agree.   *Aḥṭmpshn* (אהטמפשן)

If you propose to her, she will agree, but not her relatives.   *Bvyntz'hp* (בוינצחף)

She does not want you, but her relatives do.   *Gzksqktz* (גזכסקדץ)

She and her relatives do not want you.   *Dhl'arm* (דחלערם)

6

Go to the prince without fear, for he will honor you.   *Aḥṭmpshn* (אהטמפשן)

Go to the prince if you want; no harm   *Bvyntz'hp* (בוינצחף)

will occur to you.

If you go, you will lose money but attain your request.   *Gzksqktz* (גזכסקדץ)

If you go, you will lose money for no purpose.   *D'hl'arm* (דחלערם)

7

Know that oil will devalue greatly this year.   *Azmqn* (אזמקן)

This year it will devalue a bit.   *B'hnrp* (בחנרף)

This year it will remain stable.   *Gṯsshtz* (גטסשץ)

This year it will increase a bit.   *Dy'at* (דיעת)

This year it will increase greatly.   *Hkpk* (הכפך)

This year the olives will yield a lot of oil.   *Vltzm* (ולצם)

8

Trust in God, for there are no robbers on this road.   *Azmqn* (אזמקן)

There are robbers, but they will not come out.   *B'hnrp* (בחנרף)

If you stay here one more week, they will leave.   *Gṯshstz* (גטששץ)

There are robbers on the way that will dispossess you.   *Dy'at* (דיעת)

Know that they take people as slaves.   *Hkpk* (הכפך)

Don't go; these people are murderers, and they will kill you.   *Vltzm* (ולצם)

[23]

9

Know that he indulged in pederasty.	*Alk* (אלך)
He committed adultery.	*Bmm* (במם)
He slept with his wife while she was menstruate.	*Gnn* (גנן)
He slept with a gentile woman.	*Dsp* (דסף)
He slept with a maidservant.	*H'atz* (העץ)
He slept with a betrothed girl.	*Vyp* (ויפ)
He transgressed with one of the fifteen forbidden women.	*Ztz* (זצ)
He desecrated God's name publicly.	*'hqr* (חקר)
He ate forbidden meats.	*Tr* (טר)
He ate from unclean animals.	*Ysh* (יש)
He is a murderer.	*Kt* (כת)

10

Know that the king of Edom wins this year.	*A'hst* (אחסת)
The king of Edom will win but have many slain.	*Bt'ak* (בטעך)
The king of France will win without casualties.	*Gyps* (גיפם)
The king of France will win but lose many soldiers.	*Dktzl* (דכצל)
No one will be vanquished this year.	*Hlqp* (הלקף)
The king of Edom will win on the field, but the fort will not fall.	*Vmrtz* (ומרץ)

The king of France will win on the field,   *Znsh* (זנש)
but the fort will not fall.

11

This city is good for you, stay there.   *Avk'ashp* (אוכעשף)

This city is good for you now, but it will   *Blpttz* (בזלפתץ)
turn bad soon.

This city is neither good nor bad; you   *Ghmtzk* (גחמצך)
may stay there.

This city is bad now, but soon it will turn   *Dnqs* (דטנקס)
good for you.

[24] Leave this city, for it is bad for you.   *Hsrn* (היסרן)

12

It would be profitable for you to look for   *Ahṭmpshn* (אהטמפשן)
a friend.

It is better to stay alone, for your luck is   *Bvyntztp* (בוינצתף)
good.

If you take a friend, you will neither lose   *Gzksqrtz* (גזכסקרץ)
nor gain.

Beware not to take a friend, for you will   *D'hl'arm* (דחלערם)
lose.

13

If you want to know about some girls – let us say for example that
there are four – divide then the twenty-seven letters of the alphabet,
and start with the oldest among the girls. Throw the letters until the
twenty-seven are completed. Then, open the book as known, and
the girl who falls in the portion of the fiftieth letter of the lottery, you

shall take for a wife. Use this method starting with two girls, and up to one-hundred.

14

Is it good not to divorce your wife.   *Ahtmpshn* (אהטמפשן)

If you want a divorce for lack of children,   *Bvyntztp* (בוינצתף)
you are the cause.

If you divorce her your luck will turn   *Gzksqktz* (גזכסקרץ)
bad.

It is good for you to divorce her.   *D'hl'arm* (דחלערם)

15

This wealth will stand for a long time;   *Avk'ashp* (אוכעשף)
you can trust in it.

You will lose it. Perform charity; perhaps   *Bzlpttz* (בזלפתץ)
it will remain.

This wealth will disappear, but you won't   *G'hmtzk* (גחמצך)
have to beg.

It was decreed that you will have to beg.   *Dtnqs* (דטנקס)

Do not rely on your wealth, for you will   *Hysrn* (היסרן)
die poor.

   [25]

16

Your wife will die and you will remarry.   *Avk'ashp* (אוכעשף)

You will grow old with your wife and she   *Bzlpttz* (בזלפתץ)
will die before you.

You will die in the same week, but she   *G'hmtzk* (גחמצך)

will die first.

You will die in the same month, but you will die first.   *Dṯnqs* (דטנקס)

You will die, and your wife will remarry.   *Hysrn* (היסרן)

17

The one you ask about was killed by an Ishmaelite.   *A'hst* (אחסת)

This man was killed by an uncircumcised gentile.   *Kṯ'ak* (כטעך)

This man was killed by a Jew.   *Gypm* (גיפם)

This man was devoured by a wild beast.   *Dktzn* (דכצן)

This man got sick, died on the way, and was buried there.   *Hlqp* (הלקף)

This man froze to death in the snow.   *Vmrtz* (ומרץ)

This man died suddenly.   *Znsh* (זנש)

18

Do not worry; you will have more boys and girls.   *Azmqn* (אזמקן)

Know that two sons will remain after you.   *B'hnrp* (בחנרף)

One son and one daughter will remain after you.   *Gṯsshtz* (גטסשץ)

One son will remain after you.   *Dy'at* (דיעת)

You only have this daughter.   *Hkpk* (הכפך)

You will not have children from this one; you must wed again.   *Vltzm* (ולצם)

19

This illness is from heaven.

Adzym 'aqtn
(אדזימעקתן)

This one is struck by demons and not by nature.

Bh'hknprkp
(בההחכנפרדף)

This one is struck by demons and by nature.

Gvṭlstzshstz
(גוטלסצששסץ)

[26]

20

Take that boat; you will go in peace.

Azmqn (אזמקן)

You will suffer on that boat, but you will go in peace.

B'hnrp (בחנרף)

You will meet pirates on the sea, but you will survive.

Gtsshtz (גטססשץ)

If this boat stays for ten days take it; otherwise do not.

Dy'at (דיעת)

Do not take this boat; it will be captured.

Hkpk (הכפך)

This boat will sink.

Vltzm (ולצם)

21

Trust this man; he does not mislead you.

Avk'ashp (אוכעשף)

In the past, he did not mislead you, but now he wants to.

Bzlpttz (בזלפתץ)

He does not want to mislead you, but others advise him to.

G'hmtzk (גחמצך)

He did mislead you but repented; wait

Dtnqs (דטנקס)

until he repents.

He is not faithful; he is misleading you.   *Hysrn* (היסרן)

22

Go to court and you will win.   *Aḥtmpshn* (אהטמפשן)

The judge will compromise between the   *Bvntztp* (בוינצתף)
two of you.

You will not win in court.   *Gzksqktz* (גזכסקדץ)

If you want to win you have to bribe the   *D'hl'arm* (דחלערם)
judge.

23

There will be many fruits, but they will   *Aḥtmpshn* (אהטמפשן)
be struck by hail.

There will be many fruits, but the wind   *Bvynztzp* (בוינצתף)
will make them fall.

There will be few good fruits and they   *Gzksqktz* (גזכסקדץ)
will ripen well.

This year, fruits will be light and few.   *D'hl'arm* (דחלערם)

[27]

24

If you want to know how many robbers there are, throw the lot as
mentioned and take the fiftieth letter. Start again and count the
seven times. Take the fiftieth letter; look at it, and see if it represents
a single number, a decimal number, or the hundreds. Look at the
first letter again, and see if it is the same letter, for instance *Daleth* in
both cases: then, you know for sure that there are four robbers. If
the first one is *Daleth* and the second *Mem*, there are forty-four
robbers. If the first one is *Daleth* and the second *Tav*, there are four-

hundred-four thieves. But if the first letter represents hundreds and the second tens, like *Tav* and *Mem*, there are eighty robbers. If the first lot is *Tav* and the second *Daleth*, it means that the second testifies against the first, that it is neither hundreds, nor tens, nor units, for there is a *Tav*. Rather, turn the *Tav* into a reduced number (*Mispar Qatan*), which is four, and multiply it by the second lot, four, which makes sixteen robbers. If the first letter is *Daleth* and the second *Gimel,* multiply three by four; this makes twelve. Subtract four denied from the second lot, and you obtain eight robbers. If the first is *Gimel* and the second *Daleth*, it will be six, for *Daleth* comes to add a number identical with the first one: so it makes six. The general rule is as follows: if a letter representing units comes out with the first lot, and a larger one also representing units with the second lot, just add them up. If the larger one comes out with the first lot and the smaller one with the second, multiply them and subtract the first letter that was denied. Apply this rule whether the first and the second lots are decimals or hundreds. But if the first lot is a unit and the second decimals or hundreds, add them up. And so if the first is decimals and the second hundreds, add them up and obtain your number. But if the first is units, or decimals, or hundreds, and the second identical, then the number will be like the first lot. If the first lot is *Tav* and the second *Mem*, then *Tav* leaves the category of the hundreds, becomes a decimal, and turns into forty. Then, add forty and forty in order to obtain eighty. If *Tav* comes up in the first lot and *Nun* in the second one, then the second teaches about the first that it is not among the hundreds, but among the decimals. So, the first is forty and the second fifty, [28] and they have to be added: forty and fifty makes ninety. Following this system, you will understand everything from the numbers that will come up.

25

Know that this girl is a virgin; no man has known her.   *A'ḥtmpshtz* (אהטמפשץ)

She is a virgin, but a man has known her.   *Bvyntztp* (בוינצתף)

She is accidentally not a virgin.   *Gzksqktz* (גזכסקדץ)

She fornicated.   *D'hl'arh* (דחלערה)

26

Reuven and Simon fight and Reuven wins.   *Adzym'atn* (אדזימעקתן)

Simon wins over Reuven.   *Bh'hknprkp* (בההחכנפרדף)

No one wins.   *Bvt̠lstzshstz* (בוטלסצששסץ)

27

This house is good for you; do not leave it.   *Aht̠mpshn* (אהטמפשן)

This house is good although sorcery is hidden in it. If you remove it, it will be very good.   *Bvyntztp* (בוינצתף)

You can leave or stay, for it is neither good or bad.   *Gzksqktz* (גזכסקדץ)

Leave this house; it is very bad for you.   *D'hl'arm* (דחלערם)

28

This partnership is very good for you.   *Avk'shp* (אוכעשף)

It is good at the moment, but later on you will lose.   *Bzlpttz* (בזלפתץ)

It has good luck, but they will transgress and you will lose.   *G'hmtzk* (גחמצך)

It is neither good nor bad; do whatever   *Dṯnqs* (דטנקס)
you want.

Do not enter this partnership; it is very   *Hysrn* (היסרן)
bad for you.

[29]

29

If you want to know which one of the boys you should take as a
son-in-law, divide the alphabet as described in paragraph 12, and
take the one who corresponds to the fiftieth letter in the book.

30

Take your deceased brother's wife to   *Aghṯkmspshkntz*
establish his name.   (אגהזטכמספפקשדזץ)

Do not take her, for she is bad for you.   *Bdv'hln'atzrtsp*
   (בדוחילנעצרתסף)

31

Take this woman; even if she is a killer,   *Adzym'aqtn*
she is your mate.   (אדזימעקתן)

Take her; your luck is strong and she will   *Bh'hknprkp*
not kill you.   (בההחכנפרדף)

Beware! Do not take her, for she will kill   *Gvṯlstzshstz*
you.   (גוטלססצששסץ)

32

Know that whoever casts on one of these letters, his star will be:

Aries for *Am"n* (אמ"ן): one shall be twice poor and rich.

Taurus for *Bn"p* (בנ"ף): one shall be sometimes poor, sometimes rich.

Gemini for *Gs"tz* (גס"ץ): one shall be wise, understanding, rich, trustworthy, and will marry twice.

Cancer for *D"'a* (ד"ע): one shall become rich from the woman he marries.

Lion for *H"p* (ה"פ): one shall be very rich.

Virgo for *V"tz* (ו"צ): one shall be moderately rich.

Libra for *Z"q* (ז"ק): one shall be rich and an astronomer.

Scorpio for *'h"r* (ח"ר): one shall have many children.

Sagittarius for *T"sh* (ט"ש): one shall live a transient life.

Capricorn for *Y"t* (י"ת): one shall be an important man but be moderately rich.

Aquarius for *K"d* (כ"ד): one shall be a merchant who deals faithfully.

[30] Pisces for *L"m* (ל"ם): one shall be lucky in business.

If you want to know about your children's star, cast the lot as mentioned and see which letter is the fiftieth. That letter corresponds to his star.

33

Know that all your brothers will get married. *Ahtmpshn* (אהטמפשן)

Only one of your brothers will get married. *Bvyntztp* (בוינצתף)

All of them will marry except for one. *Gzksqktz* (גזכסקךץ)

They will all marry, but one will become a widower. *D'hl'arm* (דחלערם)

34

Your mate is in this town; look for her.	*Azmqn* (אזמקן)
She is in this town. Wait a bit; she will come by herself.	*B'hnrp* (בחנרף)
She is not yet in town, but she will come.	*Gtsshtz* (גטסשץ)
Look for her in another town.	*Dy'at* (דיעת)
She is not in this country, but in another land.	*Hkpk* (הכפך)
She is one of the fifteen forbidden women; pray for another one.	*Vltzm* (ולצם)

35

The one who strikes this man is a Jewish *Ruach*.	*Azmqn* (אזמקן)
The one who strikes this man is an Ishmaelite *Ruach*.	*B'hnrp* (בחנרף)
[31] The one who strikes this man is an uncircumcised *Ruach*.	*Gtsshtz* (גטסשץ)
It is a Jewish demon.	*Dy'at* (דיעת)
It is an Ishmaelite demon.	*Hkpk* (הכפך)
It is an uncircumcised demon.	*Vltzm* (ולצם)

36

You will not suffer on the sea at all.	*Avkshp* (אוכעשף)
You will suffer but not very much.	*Bzlpttz* (בזלפתץ)
You will suffer much, but you will be safe with no damage.	*G'hmtzk* (גחמצך)

You will suffer much; everything will be thrown in the sea, but you will be safe. *Dṯnqm* (דטנקם)

You will suffer much and the boat will be destroyed. *Hysrn* (היסרן)

37

Know that this man did not steal anything from you. *Avk'ashp* (אוכעשף)

This man did not steal but planned the theft. *Bzlpttz* (בזלפתץ)

He did not steal and did not plan, but he knew about the theft. *G'hmtzk* (גחמצך)

He did not steal, but he is involved and receives a part. *Dṯnqs* (דטנקס)

This man is the thief himself. *Hysrn* (היסרן)

38

The deal you are thinking about will succeed and not fail. *Adzym 'aqtn* (אדזימעקתן)

This deal has profit and loss. *Bh'hknprkp* (בההכנפרדף)

It has loss and no profit. *Gvṯlstzshstz* (גוטלסצששסץ)

39

This year is good for all seeds. *Ahṯmpshn* (אהטממפשן)

This year is good for spring seeds but not for stalk seeds. *Bvyntztp* (בוינצתף)

[32] This year is bad for spring seeds but good for stalk seeds.   *Gzksqktz* (גזכסקדץ)

This year is bad for all seeds.   *D'hl'arm* (דחלערם)

40

The man you asked about lives happily.   *Azmqn* (אזמקן)

This man lives but is sad because of financial loss.   *B'hnrp* (בחנרף)

The man is sick; he is mourning but will heal.   *Gtsshtz* (גטססשץ)

He is alive but deadly sick.   *Dy'at* (דיעת)

The man is dead and left a lot of money.   *Hkpk* (הכפך)

The man died in poverty.   *Vltzm* (ולצם)

   If you want to know how much money, calculate as we have done concerning robbers in paragraph 24. Follow this method for all questions addressed to you.

41

Her husband did not fornicate; let her heart be confident.   *Ahtmpshn* (אהטמפשן)

He is ready to fornicate, but has not done so.   *Bvntztp* (בוינצתף)

He did fornicate, but under a magic spell.   *Gzksqktz* (גזכסקדץ)

He did fornicate and will continue so.   *D'hl'arm* (דחלערם)

This year, the Arabs will not overtake the great army.   *Ak'ashp* (אכעשף)

There will be a great war between them; the great army will win, and they will   *Bzlpttz* (בזלפתתץ)

lack nothing.

The Arabs will attack the great army without winning, but they shall take bounty from them.   *G'hmtzk* (גחמצך)

The Arabs shall conquer the great army and take a big bounty.   *Dtnqs* (דטנקס)

Many Arabs will overtake the great army, and nothing shall remain.   *Hysm* (היסרן)

43

Go where you think you have lost that object and find it there.   *Avk'ashp* (אוכעשף)

It is not where you think it is; search and you will find it.   *Bzlpttz* (בזלפתץ)

Remember where it was and you will find it.   *G'hmtzk* (גחמצך)

[33] Someone took it; make an announcement and you will find it.   *Dtnqs* (דטנקס)

An evil man took it, and he will never give it back.   *Hysm* (היסרן)

44

Your friends are trustworthy; they did not cheat you.   *Ahtmpshn* (אהטמפשן)

They are cheating you, but others are not aware of it.   *Bvntztp* (בוינצתף)

They did not cheat you yet, but they will.   *Gzksqktz* (גזכסקדץ)

Beware of them; they are cheating you.   *D'hl'arm* (דחלערם)

If you want to know which ones are cheating you, divide the twenty-seven letters of the alphabet, etc., as in paragraph 13.

45

Take this bridegroom; he is good for you and for your daughter.   *A'hst* (אחסת)

He has good luck, but he will be wicked with your daughter.   *Bṯ'ak* (בטעך)

He is rich now, but after his marriage, he will become poor.   *Gypm* (גיפם)

Do not fall for his looks, because later he will rebel.   *Tktzn* (דכצן)

He is good, but he will die right after the wedding.   *Hlqp* (הלקף)

Do not take him.   *Vmrtz* (ומרץ)

If you take him, your daughter will die that same year.   *Znsh* (זנש)

46

The slave who escaped will return soon.   *Adzm'aqtn* (אדזימעקתן)

Your slave did not escape but was taken as a captive.   *Bh'hknprkp* (בההחכנפרךף)

The slave who escaped will not return.   *Gvṯlstzshstz* (גוטלסצששסץ)

47

Know that so and so only thinks good of   *Avk'ashp* (אוכעשף)

you.

So and so does not think bad about you.   *Bzlpttz* (בזלפתץ)

[34] So and so thinks good and bad about you, but he has scruples; go and appease him.   *G'hmtzk* (גחמצך)

So and so does not think bad, but his advisors force him to do so.   *Dṭnqs* (דטנקס)

Beware of so and so, for all his thoughts about you are bad.   *Hysrn* (היסרן)

48

This betrothal is good and will come to a good end.   *Avk'ashp* (אוכעשף)

It is good; there will be fighting, but it will come to a good end.   *Bzlpttz* (בזלפתץ)

It will not materialize because of the bridegroom.   *Ghmtzk* (גחמצך)

This betrothal is not from heaven but comes from sorcery.   *Dṭnqs* (דטנקס)

This betrothal is very bad.   *Hysrn* (היסרן)

49

Do not change the store; it is good for you.   *Aḥtmpshn* (אהטמפשן)

Do not change the store; soon everything will turn for the better.   *Bvyntztp* (בוינצתף)

This store has an average luck; you decide what to do.   *Gzksqktz* (גזכסקדץ)

Leave this store; it is bad for you.   *D'hl'ars* (דחלערס)

50

If you want to know how many years you will live, cast one and then a second lot, as described in paragraph 24, but the calculation will be different. If a unit, from one to nine, comes up – for example, if three comes up first and then seven – multiply them and obtain twenty-one. But if seven comes first and then three, you only obtain ten. This is the method for single units. If three comes up at first and then thirty, you obtain thirty-three. But if thirty comes up first and then three, you subtract three from thirty and obtain twenty-seven. This is the method for a combination of units and [35] tens. Know also that any letter representing hundreds will only count as tens, and if one of the hundreds comes up first followed by units, follow the method described for tens and units. But if the tens come first, like forty, followed by hundreds, like four hundred, you then obtain eighty years. If one of the tens comes up first, like seventy, and then one of the hundreds, like two-hundred [*Kaf* as an end consonant], eighty [*Pe* as an end consonant], nine-hundred [*Tzade* as an end consonant], then the hundreds become tens and the tens units. For example, if ninety comes up first, and then nine-hundred, then nine-hundred becomes ninety, ninety becomes nine, and thus you obtain ninety-nine years. If both times the numbers are equal, follow the first number, without adding or subtracting. If the person who asks has passed his teens, and three comes up first and then two, tell him that he has three years to live. This is the method for any number that is less than the years of the one who asks: you add that number to his years.

51

This patient will heal with an amulet; I approve the physician and the amulet.
     Avk'ashk (אוכעשך)

This amulet is good but not for this patient.
     Bzlptn (בזלפתן)

This patient will heal with this amulet.
     Q'hmtzm (קחממצם)

This patient will be healed by doctors, not by an amulet.	*Dṯnqp* (דטנקף)
This patient has no cure whatsoever.	*Hysrn* (היסרן)

52

You can be sure that there will not be pirates at the sea.	*Avk'ashp* (אוכעשף)
There are pirates, but they will pursue you without success.	*Bzlpttz* (בזלפתץ)
When they approach, a storm will come and save you.	*G'hmtzk* (גחממצך)
They will take the boat, but you will escape on a small vessel.	*Dṯnqs* (דטנקס)
They will reach you and you will not be able to escape.	*Hysrn* (היסרן)

[36]

53

The thief is one of your children.	*Ayq* (איק)
It is one of your brothers.	*Bkr* (בכר)
It is one of your servants.	*Glsh* (גלש)
It is one of your relatives.	*Dmt* (דמת)
It is one of the relatives of your wife.	*Hnk* (הנך)
It is one of the relatives of your children.	*Vsm* (וסם)
It is one of your relatives who visits your house.	*Z'an* (זען)
It is one of the guests.	*'hpp* (חפף)
It is an anonymous person.	*Ṭtztz* (טצץ)

If you want to know who is the thief, divide all the above-mentioned according to the alphabet and cast the lot. The one on whom the lot falls is the thief.

54

Do not fear this killer; he will die and you will be safe.	*Avk'ashp* (אוכעשף)
He will go to war and forget about you.	*Bzlpttz* (בזלפתץ)
Do not fear him, he is going to war and will die there.	*G'hmtzk* (גחמצך)
Do not fear him; he will soon fall and you will be safe.	*Dṯnqs* (דטנקס)
Run away, for you are not safe here.	*Hysrn* (היסרן)

55

Wheat and other grains will devalue this year.	*Avk'ashp* (אוכעשף)
Wheat will devalue, but other grains will rise.	*Bzlpttz* (בזלפתץ)
Wheat will rise, but other grains will devalue.	*G'hmtzk* (גחמצך)
Wheat and other grains will rise a bit.	*Dṯnqs* (דטנקס)
Wheat and other grains will rise a lot.	*Hysrn* (היסרן)

[37]

56

The one you asked about is alive.	*Ahṯmpshn* (אהטמפשן)
He was neither killed nor captured.	*Bvyntztp* (בוינצתף)

He was struck with a sword but did not die.   *Gzksqktz* (גזכסקקדץ)

He was indeed killed.   *D'hl'ars* (דחלערס)

57

Tell this lady that her husband does not desire any woman.   *Aḥtmpshn* (אהטמפשן)

Let her watch that he is not seduced.   *Bvyntztp* (בוינצתף)

He desires a woman, for he is under a spell.   *Gzksqktz* (גזכסקקדץ)

Her husband desires women because of his lust.   *D'hl'ars* (דחלערס)

58

This prisoner will come out without any loss.   *Azmqn* (אזמקן)

He will come out with a loss.   *B'hnrp* (בחנרף)

He will remain in jail but will come out for free.   *Gṭsshtz* (גטסשץ)

He will remain in jail, lose money and come out.   *Dy'at* (דיעת)

He will die in jail.   *Hpkk* (הפכך)

He will come out to be executed.   *Vltzs* (ולצס)

59

Your star is Saturn.   *A'hst* (אחסת)

Your star is Jupiter.   *Bṭ'ask* (בטעסך)

Your star is Mars.	*Gyps* (גיפס)
Your star is the Sun.	*Dktzn* (דכצן)
Your star is Venus.	*Hlqp* (הלקף)
Your star is Mercury.	*Vmrtz* (ומרץ)
Your star is the Moon.	*Znsh* (זנש)

[38]

60

If you want to know who among the friends is the thief, see how many they are, divide the alphabet as mentioned above. The letter on which the lot falls is the thief.

61

This bridegroom is good for your daughter.	*Azmqn* (אזמקן)
He is good, for he is peaceful, but they will be poor.	*B'hnrp* (בחנרף)
He is good, but she will become a widow.	*Gṭsshtz* (גטסשץ)
He is good, but she will have no children from him.	*Dy'at* (דיעת)
He is good, but he will divorce her in the future.	*Hkpk* (הכפך)
Do not take him, for he is very bad for your daughter.	*Vltzs* (ולצס)

62

Send for this slave wherever you think; he is there.	*Adz'hym 'aqtn* (אדזחימעקתן)

If you think that he is in the west, he is in the east.   *Bh'hknprkp* (בההחכנפרדף)

Do not look for him; you will not catch him.   *Gvṯlstzshstz* (גוטלסצשסץ)

If you want to know which way he escaped, see how many ways there are, divide the alphabet accordingly, start the letter *Alef* with the east, *Beit* with the south, *Gimel* with the west and *Daleth* with the north, etc.; the letter on which the lot falls is the way of his escape.

63

Marry this widow right away.   *Ahst* (אחסת)

Her mate is married; after the death of his wife he will marry her.   *Bṯ'ak* (בטעך)

Her mate is not in town, he will come soon.   *Gyps* (גיפס)

[39] She has no luck in this town; she will find her mate somewhere else.   *Dktzn* (דכצן)

Her mate is overseas; he will come and marry her.   *Hlqp* (הלקף)

She is a killer; the first one was her husband.   *Vmrtz* (ומרץ)

She will never marry again.   *Znsh* (זנש)

64

If you want to know under which good star this betrothal should be made, cast the lot as in paragraph 32, and on whatever star it falls, you shall conclude it.

65

Go into this partnership, you will profit from it.   *A'htmpshn* (אהטמפשן)

Go into partnership but not with these people.   *Bvytztp* (בוינצתף)

Go into partnership as you wish.   *Gzksqktz* (גזכסקדץ)

Refrain from any partnership.   *D'hl'ars* (דחלערס)

66

If you want to know how many children one will have, cast the lot and look at the fiftieth letter. If it is a unit and the second lot is identical, he will have as many children as the first number. If the second number is of the tens, reduce it to a smaller number (*Mispar Qatan*) and add the first number: that is the number of his children. But if both the first and the second numbers are of the tens and the first is greater, you only consider the second. If they are equal, you consider only the first one. But if the second is greater, add the second to [40] the first, and that is the number of children. The same rule applies to hundreds. Know that when it comes to children, tens and hundreds represent units. When both numbers are units, like four for the first lot and six for the second, this makes only six children. We do not add the first number to the second, since the second lot confirms the units, for if you add six to four, you obtain ten.

67

Children die because of her [bad] luck.   *A'hst* (אחסת)

They die because of the bad absorption, in Arabic, *El Qarinah*.   *Bt'ak* (בטעך)

They die because of this house; leave it and they will live.   *Gps* (גפס)

They die because of this town; leave it and they will live.	*Dktzn* (דכצן)
They die because of your [bad] luck.	*Hlqp* (הלקף)
They die because of sorcery.	*Vmrtz* (ומרץ)
They die because of sin.	*Znsh* (זנש)

68

The rumor you heard is true.	*Ahtmpshn* (אהטמפשן)
The rumor is partly true and partly false.	*Bvyntztp* (בוינצתף)
It is something else, and the opposite of this.	*Gzksqktz* (גזכסקדץ)
This rumor is a complete lie.	*D'hl'ars* (דחלערס)

69

The thief is a man.	*Ahtmpshn* (אהטמפשן)
The thief is a woman.	*Bvyntztp* (בוינצתף)
It is a boy without a beard.	*Gzksqktz* (גזכסקדץ)
It is a young virgin.	*D'hl'ars* (דחלערס)

[41]

70

Run away; they will not pursue you.	*Avk'ashp* (אוכעשף)
Run away; even if they purse you, they will not catch you.	*Bzlpttz* (בזלפתץ)
Do not run away, for they will catch you; hide in the town.	*Ghmtzk* (גחמצך)

Do not run away and hide, lest they find you and you lose money.   *Dṯnqs* (דטנקס)

Do not run away and hide, for they will find you and kill you.   *Hysrn* (היסרן)

71

This year the rains will fill up cisterns, pits, and caves.   *Azmqn* (אזמקן)

There will be just enough rain for cisterns.   *B'hnrp* (בחנרף)

There will be rain for cisterns at the beginning of the winter.   *Gṯsshtz* (גטסשיץ)

There will be just enough rain for the seeds.   *Dy'at* (דיעת)

There will be cistern water only in the middle of the winter.   *Hkpk* (הכפך)

There will be a drought this year.   *Vltzm* (ולצם)

72

If you look for him, you will find him in the field between the trees.   *Avk'ashp* (אוכעשף)

The slain man lies between the trees, far from the road.   *Bzlpttz* (בזלפתץ)

He lies by the riverside.   *G'hmtzk* (גחמצך)

He was buried by the robbers.   *Dṯnqs* (דטנקס)

They threw him in the water.   *Hysrn* (היסרן)

73

You can be sure that your wife did not fornicate.   *Aḥtmpshn* (אהטמפשן)

She did not fornicate, but she wants to.   *Bvyntztp* (בוינצתף)

She fornicated against her will.   *Gzksqktz* (גזכסקדץ)

She fornicated willingly.   *D'hl'ars* (דחלערס)

[42]

74

The prince wants to take your money and then free you.   *A'hst* (אחסת)

He wants to whip you, take your money, and then free you.   *Bṯ'ak* (בטעך)

He wants to whip you badly, and then free you.   *Gyps* (גיפס)

He wants to kill you by the sword.   *Dktzn* (דכצן)

He wants to hang you.   *Hlqp* (הלקף)

He wants to put you up on a tree.   *Vmrtz* (ומרץ)

He wants to take revenge on you.   *Znsh* (זנש)

75

The last Messiah is already born; he walks among us.   *Avk'ashp* (אוכעשף)

The Messiah of the end of days is born.   *Bzlpttz* (בזלפתץ)

[43] The mother of the Messiah is pregnant with the savior of Israel.   *G'hmtzk* (גחמצך)

His mother will soon be pregnant with him.   *Dṯnqs* (דטנקס)

The Messiah is far from being born.   *Hysrn* (היסרן)

76

The theft will be found in time.   *Avk'ashp* (אוכעשף)

The theft will be sold this week.   *Bzlpttz* (בזלפתץ)

It was sent to be sold in another town.   *G'hmtzk* (גחמצך)

It was sold yesterday.   *Dtnqs* (דטנקס)

It was sold and the money was spent.   *Hysrn* (היסרן)

77

This gem is very good.   *Ahtmmpshn* (אהטמפשן)

It is good, but it has a flaw; look and you shall find it.   *Bvyntztp* (בוינצתף)

It is mediocre.   *Gzksqktz* (גזכסקדץ)

It is just a piece of glass.   *D'hl'ars* (דחלערם)

78

This slave hides in town; he will only escape in a while.   *Avk'ashp* (אוכעשף)

He is in town. He will escape this week; watch and you will find him.   *Bzlpttz* (בזלפתץ)

He escaped yesterday; pursue him, you will find him on the road.   *Ghmtzk* (גחמצך)

He left the town and hides in a village.   *Dtnqs* (דטנקס)

He ran away, and you will not be able to   *Hysrn* (היסרן)

find him.

79

God willing, this betrothal will be concluded right away.   *Azmqn* (אזמקן)

It will be done but with difficulty.   *B'hnrp* (בחנרף)

[44] It will be done but cancelled later.   *G̱tsshtz* (גטסשץ)

It will not be done, but another one will be concluded instead.   *Dy'at* (דיעת)

As you are thinking of this other one, it will be annulled, and the first one will come through.   *Hpkk* (הפכך)

Do not think about this betrothal; it will not happen.   *Vltzm* (ולצם)

80

Conclude this betrothal on Sunday.   *Ahst* (אחסת)

Conclude this betrothal on Monday.   *Bṯ'ak* (בטעך)

Conclude this betrothal on Tuesday.   *Gyps* (גיפם)

Conclude this betrothal on Wednesday.   *Dktzn* (דכצן)

Conclude this betrothal on Thursday.   *Hlqp* (הלקף)

Conclude this betrothal on Friday.   *Vmrtz* (ומרץ)

Conclude this betrothal on Saturday.   *Znsh* (זנש)

81

If you want to know which one to take among the slaves, find out how many they are, divide the alphabet accordingly, cast lots and take the slave on which the lot falls. Follow that method for animals and maidservants; and thus, you shall know what to buy.

82

The man who drowned in the sea swam and was saved.   *Ahtmpshn* (אהטממפשן)

He will miraculously find a tree and float away.   *Bvintztp* (בוינצתף)

He is dead and they will find him on the shore.   *Gzksqktz* (גזכסקקדץ)

He was eaten by fish.   *D'hl'arm* (דחלערם)

83

Do not prepare a medicine; she will soon be pregnant.   *A* (א)

Do not prepare a medicine; she is fine, but her husband is not.   *B* (ב)

[45] She is preventing it; prepare a medicine, and she will get pregnant.   *G* (ג)

She is prevented because of demons.   *D* (ד)

She will not get pregnant for a long time; no need for a medicine.   *H* (ה)

She is barren every seven years.   *V* (ו)

She is barren and will not have a child.   *Z* (ז)

She is prevented because of witchcraft.   *'h* (ח)

84

This boat did not go out but will be much delayed.   *Aḥtmpshn* (אהטמפשן)

It will go out this week with a good wind.   *Bvintztp* (בוינצתף)

It already went out and will come rapidly.   *Gzksqktz* (גזכסקדץ)

It already went out but was delayed somewhere else.   *D'hl'arm* (דחלערם)

85

The thief is Jewish.   *Azmqn* (אזמקן)

He is an apostate.   *B'hnrp* (בחנרף)

He is an Ishmaelite.   *Gṭsshtz* (גטסשץ)

He is uncircumcised but became an Ishmaelite.   *Dy'at* (דיעת)

He is an Arab.   *Hkpk* (הכפך)

He is uncircumcised.   *Vltzm* (ולצם)

If you want to know which one is among the uncircumcised, divide the alphabet according to their kinds in the city, and cast the lot as usual; the one on which the letter falls belongs to that group.

86

Nothing will happen to this newborn; he will grow and live.   *Avk'ashp* (אוכעשף)

His star is gainful; do not leave him alone, lest Lilith kills him.   *Bzlptz* (בזלפתץ)

[46] Do not leave him alone; he is in danger for three years.   *G'hmtzk* (גחממצך)

Watch him during the eight days of circumcision; he could be killed.   *Dṯnqs* (דטנקס)

It is impossible to save him from Lilith.   *Hysrn* (היסרן)

87

This house has luck; it will bring you richness and honor.   *Aḥṯmpshn* (אהטמפשן)

Take it; you will find a precious thing in it.   *Bvntztp* (בוינצתף)

You may take it; you will not lose.   *Gzksqktz* (גזכסקדץ)

Do not take it; it has bad luck, and you will lose your money.   *D'hl'arm* (דחלערם)

88

If you want to know which field to take, divide the alphabet according to their direction in the world; assign *Alef* to the east, *Beit* to the south, *Gimel* to the west and *Daleth* to the north. Then, cast the lot as usual and take the field upon which the letter shall fall.

89

Your wife is chaste; no man desires her.   *Aḥṯmpshn* (אהטמפשן)

She is chaste, but watch her since some are chasing her.   *Bvyntztp* (בוינצתף)

She desires love, not fornication.   *Gzksqktz* (גזכסקדץ)

She desires fornication.   *D'hl'arm* (דחלערם)

90

Do not hide or fear; stand before the prince, and you will succeed.   *Aḥtmpshn* (אהטמפשן)

Do not hide or fear, but if you lose money you will be saved.   *Bvyntztp* (בוינצתף)

Do not go to the prince unless you bribe the governor.   *Gzksqktz* (גזכסקדץ)

Do not go, for even if you pay, you are not safe.   *D'hl'arm* (דחלערם)

[47]

91

Your mate is in this country and will come soon.   *A'hst* (אחסת)

She is in this country, but she is too young.   *Bṭ'ak* (בטעך)

She is not in this country, but she will come soon.   *Gyps* (גיפס)

She is not in this country, but she will come later.   *Dktzn* (דכצן)

She is not here and she will not come; go and find her.   *Hlqp* (הלקף)

She is in another country; go and find her.   *Vmrtz* (ומרץ)

She is forbidden to you; pray and God will send another one.   *Znsh* (זנש)

92

The theft is in the house of the thief.   *Ayq* (איק)

It is in the house of one of his close neighbors.	*Bkr* (בכר)
It is buried in the ground of his courtyard.	*Glsh* (גלש)
It is either in the house of his brother or in the house of his friend.	*Dmt* (דמת)
It is in one of the houses of his children.	*Hnk* (הנך)
It is in one of the houses of his relative.	*Vsm* (וסם)
It is either in the house of his father or in the house of his uncle or his advisor.	*Z'an* (זען)
The theft is hidden in a cave outside the city.	*'hpp* (חפף)
The theft is not in his house but in another one in the city.	*Ttztz* (טצץ)

If you want to know in which house in the city [it is found], look further in paragraph 165, and divide the houses of the city accordingly. If you want to know which one among the above ones, such as brothers, relatives, or sons, see on which house the lot falls, and see how many persons there are in it. Divide the alphabet accordingly; the theft is found by the one on which the lot will fall.

93

If you want to know which house to take, divide the alphabet according to the number of houses, as described in paragraph 88 for fields, and cast the lot. Take the house on which the lot will fall.

[48]

94

Throw your net, and you will catch a lot of fish.	*Avk'ashp* (אוכעששף)
Wait for two hours; then, throw and you will catch.	*Bzlpttz* (בזלפתץ)

Your net will not bring up very many fish.	G'hmtzk (גחמצך)
It will only bring up a little bit.	Dṯnqs (דטנקס)
It will not bring anything.	Hysrn (היסרן)

95

This woman is the wife of this man.	Ahṯmpshn (אהטמפשן)
She is the wife of his brother.	Bvyntztp (בוינצתף)
He has nothing to do with her.	Gzksqktz (גזכסקדץ)
She will be yours after she becomes a widow.	D'hl'arm (דחלערם)

96

If you want to know which day of the week is good to enter a partnership, look in paragraph 80, and whatever day is good for betrothal is also good for partnership.

97

She is pregnant with a boy.	Aṯpn (אטפן)
She is pregnant with a girl.	Bytzp (ביצף)
She is pregnant with a boy and a girl.	Qkqtz (קכקץ)
She is pregnant with two boys.	Dlr (דלר)
She is pregnant with a child of unknown sex.	Hmsh (המש)
She is pregnant with a hermaphrodite.	Vnt (ונת)
She is pregnant with a *Ruach*.	Zsk (זסך)

She is not pregnant, but her menstruation   *'h'am* (חעם)
stopped.

[49]

98

If you want to know what death one will die, cast the lot. Take the
fiftieth letter, his name, and the name of his mother. Put them
together and divide the outcoming number in fifteen lines. Start
with the first and end with the last, and start again. Wherever
number you will reach, that will be his death.

He will fall by the sword in the war.	He will die by stoning.
He will die by fire.	He will die by hanging.
He will die on a tree.	He will die by blowing.
He will be torn by a wild beast.	He will die from a snake's bite.
He will drown in the sea.	
He will die from hailstone.	He will die by the sword.
He will die suddenly.	He will die the hard death of the wicked.
He will die like the righteous.	He will die a natural death.

99

If you want to know from which illness one will die, cast the lot.
The fiftieth letter is the illness he will die from. They are arranged
before you.

He will die from suffering.	*A* (א)
He will die from malaria.	*B* (ב)
He will die from quartan fever.	*G* (ג)
He will die from measles.	*D* (ד)

He will die from smallpox.	*H* (ה)
He will die from a plague.	*V* (ו)
He will die from plain illness.	*Z* (ז)
He will die from his lifestyle.	*'h* (ח)
He will die from old age.	*Ṯ* (ט)
He will die from jaundice.	*Y* (י)
He will die from a malign fever.	*K* (כ)
He will die from a head sickness.	*L* (ל)
[50] He will die from a heart illness.	*M* (מ)
He will die from the flank.	*N* (נ)
He will die from a blood illness.	*S* (ס)
He will die from lack of evacuation.	*'a* (ע)
He will die from leprosy.	*P* (פ)
He will die from syphilis.	*Tz* (צ)
He will die from age [the conclusion of his cycle].	*Q* (ק)
He will die from the pains of custody.	*R* (ר)
He will die because of evil forces.	*Sh* (ש)
He will die of consternation.	*T* (ת)
He will die of grief.	*K* (ך)
He will die from the evil eye.	*S* (ס)
He will die from colic.	*N* (ן)
He will die from fright.	*P* (ף)
He will die a natural death.	*Tz* (ץ)

100

The dream you dreamed is true.	*Azmqn* (אזמקן)
The good in it is true; the evil is false.	*B'hnrp* (בחנרף)
The evil in it is true; the good is false.	*Gṭsshtz* (גטסששץ)
It is altogether false.	*Dy'at* (דיעת)
The beginning and the end are false; the middle is true.	*Hkpk* (הכפך)
The beginning and the end are true; the middle is false.	*Vltzm* (ולצם)

101

This dream will come true within a year, i.e. twelve months.

Most of the time, this dream will come true, within twenty-five months.

[51] If the lot indicates that the dream will come true within the year and you want to know which month, organize the months starting from *Nisan* until *Adar*, and divide the alphabet accordingly. The month on which the lot falls is the one in which the dream will come true. If you want to know which year among the twenty-two years, divide the alphabet accordingly and cast the lot. The year on which the lot falls is the year in which the dream will come true.

102

This dream looks good and is good.	*Aḥtmpshn* (אהטממפשן)
It looks bad, but it is good.	*Bvyntztp* (בוינצתף)
It looks bad but it is neutral.	*Gzksqktz* (גזכסקקץ)
It looks bad and it is bad.	*D'hl'arm* (דחלערם)

103

You will attain this position easily, and you will keep it.   *Azmqn* (אזמקן)

You will attain it with difficulty, but you will keep it.   *B'hnrp* (בחנרף)

You will attain it easily, but you will not be able to keep it.   *Gtsshtz* (גטססשץ)

You will attain it with difficulty, but you will not be able to keep it.   *Dy'at* (דיעת)

You will lose a lot of money, and you will not be able to attain it.   *Hkpk* (הכפך)

You will put yourself in danger, but you will not attain it.   *Vltzm* (ולצם)

104

This position is good for you but bad for your children, who will die from the evil eye.   *Ahtmpshn* (אהטמפשן)

It is not good for you, and you will lose a lot of money.   *Bvyntztp* (בוינצתף)

This position will cause your death.   *Gzksqktz* (גזכסקדץ)

This position is very good for you.   *D'hl'arm* (דחלערם)

[52]

105

You will obtain that which you desire; just trust in God.   *Avk'ashp* (אוכעשף)

You will obtain it with a lot of money.   *Bzlpttz* (בזלפתץ)

You will obtain it with great trouble.   *G'hmtzk* (גחמצך)

You will not obtain it, even with a lot of money. *Dtnqs* (דטנקס)

You will endanger yourself without attaining it. *Hysrn* (היסרן)

106

That which you desire is very good for you. *Ahtmpshn* (אהטמפשן)

It is good for your wealth but not for your children. *Bvntztp* (בוינצתף)

You will lose a lot of money because of it. *Gzksqktz* (גזכסקקדץ)

You will endanger yourself for it. *D'hl'ars* (דחלערם)

107

Do not vouch for this, but do not worry: you will gain. *Adzym 'aqtn* (אדזימעקתן)

Vouch for this boat, and despite the trouble you will gain. *Bh'hknprtztz* (בההחכנפרץף)

Do not vouch for that boat; you will lose your money. *Gvtlstzshstz* (גוטלסצששסץ)

108

This boat will arrive peacefully without trouble. *Azmqn* (אזמקן)

It will endure much trouble at sea but come out safe. *B'hnrp* (בחנרף)

It will be pursued by enemies but will *Gtsshtz* (גטסששץ)

come out safe.

It will endure much trouble; they will throw out merchandise in the sea and you will lose out. — *Dy'at* (דיעת)

It will be taken by enemies. — *Hpk* (הכפך)

It will sink into the sea. — *Vltzm* (ולצם)

109

Do not fear to sail; it is good for you. — *Aksh* (אכש)

You will suffer, but you will be safe. — *Blt* (בלת)

[53] You will find enemies, but you will be safe. — *Gmk* (גמך)

Do not sail, for you will be taken prisoner. — *Dnm* (דנם)

Do not sail, for you will drown. — *Hsn* (הסן)

It is good for you to go by land. — *V'ap* (ועף)

It is good to go by land, but you will find robbers and will be safe. — *Zptz* (זפץ)

If you go by land, you will lose money. — *'htz* (חץ)

Do not go this way, for robbers will kill you. — *Tq* (טק)

Do not leave your house this year. — *Yr* (יר)

110

The messenger you are asking about is in town accepting his mission. — *Am* (אם)

He is accepting his mission and looking for a caravan to leave. — *B'a* (בע)

He left town and boarded a ship.	*Gp* (גפ)
He is on board but is held back, as there is no wind.	*Dtz* (דצ)
He is on board and is coming rapidly.	*Hq* (הק)
There was a storm, and he landed in another country.	*Vr* (ור)
He is still going, not yet coming back.	*Zsh* (זש)
He is not coming; he ran away.	*'ht* (חת)
He was at sea but was captured on the way back.	*Ṯk* (טך)
He was at sea but drowned on the way back.	*Ym* (ים)
He was at sea; he landed and is back.	*Kn* (כן)
He is on foot, but he ran away.	*Lp* (לף)
He is on the way, but the merchandise was stolen from him.	*Mtz* (מץ)
Robbers killed him on the way.	*K* (כ)

111

The vision he had is holy: it is from the World of Creation.	*A'hst* (אחסת)
The vision was from the World of Formation.	*Nṯ'ak* (נטעך)
[54] It was from the World of Action.	*Gyps* (גיפס)
It was from the Shell of Grief (*Qlipath Nogah*).	*Dktzn* (דכצן)
It was from the Evil Side (*Sitra A'hra*), from the Left Chariot.	*Hlkk* (הלכף)

It was from the Chariot of Haughtiness   *Vmrtz* (ומרץ)
(*Merkavath Rahab*).

It was from the World of Counter Forms   *Znsh* (זנש)
(*Olam ha-Temuroth*).

112

If you want to know under which good star to enter a partnership, cast the lot. Look at paragraph 32, and see what the fiftieth letter is. You shall enter the partnership under that star.

113

If you want to know which day to sit in the store, proceed as above.

114

If you want to know which day to enter the house, see paragraph 80, proceed as mentioned, and that will be the day to come in.

115

If you want to know which day of the month to enter the house, cast the lot and take the fiftieth letter. Then, cast a second lot, take the fiftieth letter, and put them together. Divide the out-coming number according to the days of the month you ask about. If it has thirty days, divide it accordingly, but if it is deficient, divide it in twenty-nine days. The final number is the day of the month you shall enter the house.

116

If you want to know on which day to enter the city, proceed as in paragraph 32, and you shall come in under that good star.

[55]

117

If you want to know which city is good for you to profit, write the number of the villages that you know, and cast the lot as mentioned in paragraph 115. Divide the out-coming number according to the number of villages, and the final number is the good town for you.

118

If you want to know which one among the others is a good partner for you, see how many you are thinking about, divide the alphabet accordingly, and it is the one on which the lot falls.

119

If you want to know which one among them is a bad partner, see how many you suspect, divide the alphabet accordingly, and it is the one on which the fiftieth letter falls. If there are more than twenty-seven, cast two lots and put them together as in paragraph 115. The final number is the bad one.

120

This woman is in labor, for her time has come.

This woman is in labor, for she is hungry.

She is in labor because of the cold.

It is because she carried a heavy weight.

It is because she made a vow that she did not carry out.

121

The wisdom of knowing the origin of *Nefesh* is a deep one; therefore, open your eyes and your thoughts to understand and know. Thus, you shall know what to answer to whomever asks.

[56] First of all, before you are questioned about the *Nefesh*, you have to know the name of the deceased. Cast two lots to know how many letters his name has. Put the letters together and reduce them to nine. If one is left over, his name has three letters like David (*Daleth-Vav-Daleth*). If two are left over, his name has two letters, like Gad (*Gimel-Daleth*) or Dan (*Daleth-Nun*). If three are left, the name has five letters. If four are left, the name has four letters. If five are left, the name has seven letters. If six are left, the name has six letters. If seven are left the deceased's name and first-name have nine letters, like *Chushi ha-Arki* (*'heth-Vav-Shin-Yod-He-Alef-Tesh-Khaf-Yod*), etc.; anything left less than seven is his name, without his first-name. In order to know clearly the name, you need another lot to find out his father's name. And if eight are left, his name will be composed of two [parts], his name and his first-name, and they will come together. And if nine are left, his name and first-name have eleven letters.

Now that you know how many letters the name has, I have to let you know how to bring it up in two ways:

This is the first way. If the name has two letters, you must cast two lots, with two good names. You have to pray before the Creator, and in the prayer mentioned previously, change the question and insert this request: "May it be your will, O Eternal, God of our forefathers, that I find the truth of this matter; let me know the *Nefesh* of this man about whom the lot testified, and who has such and such number of letters to his name. Let me know the truth through the lot that I will open; let the first letter of his name be without any doubt, mistake or lie. Let it be true like you who is a true God, and like your word, our king, which is true and everlasting. Let me know the second and third letters of the name, with the lot".

The person who casts the lot must have a clean body, be dressed in white and clean clothing, and must recite the prayer with full intention. Likewise, he must cast the lot at a good time and in a good day (as written in the introduction; it [57] should not be on a *Sabbath*, Tuesday, or Wednesday, and not on a cloudy day). A propitious time to cast it is on a day when the moon is rising, on a Monday at the third hour that is Jupiter, or at the tenth hour; likewise, on Thursday, at the first hour or at the eighth hour. The best time to cast is when the book of the law (*Sefer Torah*) is open for reading, at the specific day and hour.

I shall now explain the second way. If you want to know if the root of your *Neshamah* stems from ancient generations like Cain, Abel, the generation of Enosh, or that of the Flood, or that of the Dispersion, or from the Seven covenant makers; from the Tribes, from the Prophets, or from the teachers of the *Mishnah* [*Tannaim*]; from the interpreters of the *Mishnah* [*Amoraim*], or from the Gaonim [Jewish teachers from Babylon, c. 589-1038]; from the legal authorities [*Posqim*], or from the expositors of Scriptures [*Darshanim*]; from the Judges, from the kings of Judea, from the kings of Israel, or from the remnant of Israel − you must organize the names as follows:

Your *Neshamah* stems from the root of Cain.	*Atz* (אצ)
It stems from the root of Abel.	*Bq* (בק)
It stems from the generation of Enosh.	*Gr* (גר)
It stems from the generation of the Flood.	*Dsh* (דש)
It stems from the generation of the Dispersion.	*Ht* (הת)
It stems from the Seven covenants makers.	*Vk* (וך)
It stems from the Tribes.	*Sz* (זס)
It stems from the Prophets.	*'hn* (חן)

It stems from the Judges.	*Tp* (טף)
It stems from the kings of Judea.	*Ytz* (יץ)
It stems from the kings of Israel.	*K* (כ)
It stems from the *Tannaim*.	*L* (ל)
It stems from the *Amoraim*.	*M* (מ)
It stems from the *Gaonim*.	*K* (כ)
It stems from the *Posqim*.	*M* (ם)
It stems from the *Darshanim*.	*'a* (ע)
It stems from the remnant of Israel.	*P* (פ)

If you want to know now from which generation you come from, put together the letters of the first and the second casting, divide the outcome according to the above generations, and the final number is the generation you come from.

[58] And if you want to know from which limb of Cain or Abel is the root of your *Neshamah*, then divide the body according to its parts and limbs, each according to its name, from the head to the toes. Then, cast the lots as you know and put together the letter of the first lot, with the letter of the second. Divide the outcome according to the parts and limbs arranged in front of you, and the final number is the limb of the root of your *Neshamah*.

And if you want to know from which person in the generation of Enosh, then arrange in front of you all the names written from Adam to Enosh, including those of the women and the children. Then, cast the lot and put together the first and the second. Divide the outcome according to the names arranged in front of you, and the name on which it will fall is the root of your *Neshamah*.

If you want to know from the generation of Enosh until that of Noach, arrange the names as written in the *Torah*, and do as above. If you want to know from the generation of the Dispersion until Abraham, do as above. If you want to know whom among the seven covenanters, divide the alphabet among them. The first part should be empty and start with Abraham. His *Neshamah* stems from wherever the lot falls. However, if it falls on the eighth letter, it shows that his soul is not from the holy forefathers, but from the fathers of impurity and that it is reincarnated for correction.

If you want to know from which one among the tribes is the root of your *Neshamah*, divide the alphabet in thirteen parts, i.e. twelve for the tribes and an empty one. Start with Reuven until the end of the tribes, and start again. If the lot falls on the thirteenth part, it shows that it is not from the tribes, but from the chiefs of Esau and Ishmael who came to correct themselves.

If you want to know from which prophet, count all those who had the Holy Spirit (*Ruach ha-Qodesh*) in the Scriptures, except from the book of Kings and that of the Judges. Take that number, add another unit, and put together the first lot with the second. Divide the outcome according to the number in front of you with the added unit. The final number is your *Neshamah*, but if it falls on the added unit, then that *Neshamah* stems from the wordly prophets, like Balam, who came to correct himself.

[59] If you want to know from which other group your *Neshamah* stems, gather all the names of that group, and add another unit. Then, cast the lot as mentioned. If it falls on the added unit, know that you did not yet gather all the names; therefore, look for more names. After finding them, arrange them a second time and cast the lots again as above. If it falls again on the added one – and you cannot find any more names – then, bring the name up according to the first way [see the beginning of this paragraph]. You will proceed in the same fashion, with the rest of the groups. Understand this!

122

Your *Neshamah* is new; it came out now from its source.   *Azmqn* (אזמקן)

It is new, but it has dressed itself in someone else, according to the mystery of impregnation (*'ibur*).   *B'hnrp* (בהנרף)

It is new, and it came into you for its first   *Gtsshtz* (גטסשץ)

transmigration.

It already reincarnated a few times.   *Dy'at* (דיעת)

It is not new, and was only reincarnated   *Hkpk* (הכפך)
through impregnation of a few persons.

It is not a *Neshamah* but only a spark.   *Vltzm* (ולצם)

123

If you want to know how many *Mitzvot* you have to perform so as not to be reincarnated, cast two lots and put them together. The outcome represents the number of *Mitzvot* left to do. There is no need to arrange the six-hundred-thirteen *Mitzvot* in front of you for this calculation. Just look at the number: if it is less than six-hundred and thirteen, this is the number of *Mitzvot* left for you to do. But if it is greater than six-hundred-thirteen, start again over the six-hundred-thirteen *Mitzvot*, and wherever it ends, this is the amount of *Mitzvot* left to do.

If you only want to know how many positive or negative *Mitzvot*, etc., follow the same method.

[60]

124

If you want to know which *Mitzvot* you did not perform and because of which you were reincarnated, organize the two-hundred-forty-eight positive *Mitzvot* according to Maimonides, of blessed memory. Then, cast the lots with perfect intention, and put together the letters from the first and the second lots. Divide the outcome according to the positive *Mitzvot*, and add one more. The number on which it ends is the *Mitzvah* you were reincarnated for. If you want to know about another *Mitzvah*, take the first lot and cast a third one. Then, put them together and add two to the result, for this is the second time you put numbers together. Divide that number according to the two-hundred-forty-eight *Mitzvot* and the number on which it will end is the one you were reincarnated for. You shall proceed alike if you want to know about a third *Mitzvah*.

You have to cast a fourth time, put the results together, and add three, fpr this is the third time you put numbers together, and divide it according to the positive commandments as above, etc. . You shall follow this method for all positive *Mitzvot*, and add an extra number each time you put the numbers together. Understand this!

And so if you want to know about negative *Mitzvot* you must follow the above method according to the order of Maimonides. Then, you shall know which one among the negative *Mitzvot* you have to perform.

125

You reincarnated because you transgressed a positive *Mitzvah* by not doing (*be-Shev ve-'Al ta'ase*), and you are obligated to receive lashes.

You reincarnated because you transgressed a negative *Mitzvah* by actively doing (*be-Qum ve-'Ase*), and you are obligated to receive lashes.

You reincarnated because you transgressed a positive *Mitzvah* punishable by premature death (*Kareth*).

You reincarnated because you desecrated the *Sabbath* or similar forbidden acts punishable by death.

You reincarnated because you transgressed both positive and negative *Mitzvot* for which you are obligated to receive lashes.

[61] You reincarnated because you transgressed positive *Mitzvot* punishable by lashes and negative *Mitzvot* punishable by death.

You reincarnated because you transgressed negative *Mitzvot* punishable by stoning.

You reincarnated because you transgressed negative *Mitzvot* punishable by sword.

You reincarnated because you transgressed negative *Mitzvot* punishable by fire.

You reincarnated because you transgressed negative *Mitzvot* punishable by strangling.

126

If you want to know how many times you were reincarnated, cast the lots, put together the first and second letter, and divide the result in one-hundred-twenty-one. That which is left over is the number of your reincarnations. If the outcome is one hundred-twenty-one, know that it is from one-thousand-hundred-twenty-one until two-thousand.

127

If you want to know from which tribe you are, cast the lots and put together the first and the second letter. Divide the result in fifteen parts, and wherever your number ends, it will be the tribe you stem from. [Do] **like this**: From the seed of Aaron *A* (.א), from the seed of Levi *B* (.ב), from the seed of Reuven *G* (.ג), from the seed of Shimon *D* (.ד), from the seed of Yehuda *H* (.ה), from the seed of Issachar *V* (.ו), from the seed of Zebulun *Z* (.ז), from the seed of Ephraim *'h* (.ח), from the seed of Menasse *T̲* (.ט), from the seed of Benjamin *Y* (.י), from the seed of Dan *Y"a* (.יא), from the seed of Naftali *Y"b* (.יב), from the seed of Gad *Y"g* (.יג), from the seed of Asher *Y"d* (.יד), from the seed of proselytes *T̲"v* (.טו). The fruit is wherever the number ends.

128

Your mother is neither sick nor dead.	*Ah̲tmpshn* (אהטממפשן)
She is sick, but she will heal.	*Bvyntztp* (בוינצתף)
She is deathly ill.	*Gzksqktz* (גזכסקדץ)
She is already dead and buried.	*D'hl'arm* (דחלערם)

129

Your daughter did not yet give birth; her time has not come.   *Ayq* (איק)

She is in labor and will give birth rapidly.   *Bkr* (בכר)

She is in labor but having difficulties.   *Glsh* (גלש)

She gave birth and is healthy like everyone else.   *Dmt* (דמת)

She gave birth and is nearly dead because of it.   *Hnk* (הנך)

She will not give birth, for the fetus died.   *Vsm* (וסם)

She died while delivering, but the child is alive.   *Z'an* (זען)

She is alive, but the child died.   *'hpp* (חפף)

They both died.   *Ttztz* (טצץ)

130

In the future, you will receive a great inheritance.   *A'hst* (אחסת)

The inheritance will be average.   *Bt'ak* (בטעך)

An appellant will rise, and you will share it with him.   *Gypm* (גיפם)

The appellant is a close relative, and he will take it.   *Dktzn* (דכצן)

It will come to you from a distant place.   *Hlqp* (הלקף)

It will come from a distant place, but it will be hidden from you.   *Vmrtz* (ומרץ)

No inheritance will come at all.   *Znsh* (זנש)

131

If you want to know which day to travel, see paragraph 80 and go on that day.

[63]

132

If you want to know on which day to associate with someone, see paragraph 115 and associate on that day.

This man has good luck; associate with him.   *Aḥtmpshn* (אהטמפשן)

He inclines towards the good; you can associate with him.   *Bvyntztp* (בוינצתף)

His luck inclines towards the bad.   *Gzksqktz* (גזכסקדץ)

It is bad; do not associate with him, for you will lose.   *D'hl'arm* (דחלערם)

134

For your star see paragraph 32. And if you know which one among the stars is yours – such as Aries, or Taurus, etc. – look here, and see the explanation.

[♈] Male

If it is Aries, sometimes he will be rich or poor; he will fall into the hands of non-Jews or the government. He will marry, have children, and wander in distant lands. He will be good looking and lack nothing. His star shines in the sky, and whoever is born under it will be wise in business. He will be honored, go after the commandments, and shun sin, etc.; people will fight with him. He will have many enemies because of jealousy, but in the end they will fall on the ground before him, and he will rise above them. He will be in danger but will be saved. His enemies will say many things against him, but nothing will prevail. He will encounter evil for three years, but then he will find a lot of good and after hard work many riches. Then, all will love him as they love themselves. He will receive everything that he asks for from God, and much good will come to him from the star of his wife. Whoever is born under this star [Aries] will suffer from headaches, will have a blemished arm, will talk a lot, but lack nothing and end well. He has a sign on one of his thighs, and he will be ill for two years. But if he recovers the illness will return after twenty years; and, if he recovers [again], he will live until the age of eighty. Besides the sign on his thigh, he has another one on his neck [64]; his face is large, and he is rebellious. He is not afraid of anyone, and no one can defeat him.

[♈] Female

She has beautiful features and looks nice; her words are sweet and she has a sign on her head, on her face, or on her belly. Her mouth and forehead are wide; her eyelids are thick and her nostrils long; her hair is beautiful and her height pleasant. She has a skill; she helps her husband and loves him, but she loves secretly another man. Her deliveries are very painful, and in the end, she fights with her husband almost to the point of divorce. She will have pains in her body, in her joints and in her head. She always agrees with others, and her view does not stand. She will be sick at the ages of three, seven, nine, and twenty-seven, and if she survives, she will live until the age of sixty-seven. Then, she will die from the gall, or become blind and die from great pain.

[♉] Male

For Taurus, see paragraph 32. One will marry twice and have a sign on his head, on his face, or on his arm. He will speak a lot without understanding and desire things that belong to others. He will not do what he says, but people will live in peace with him. He will endure great trouble for three years, and take money that is not his. He will have children who will die. He will take women away from their husbands, and many evil things will be said daily about him and his family. He will have a blemish in his beard and will walk in many ways. These are his characteristics: he is not tall, and in the end, he will die outside of his house. He will acquire possessions like a rich house, will rise to greatness, and rise again right after falling. He will have to go through many judgments, and will father twins. He will be sick from the age of three until he is thirty-four years old and, if he survives, he will live until the age of fifty-three, or until seventy-four. He will have signs on his thumbs and knees.

[ᵇ] Female

She will be a God-fearing woman and give birth to children. She has a sign on her face, or on her belly. She is beautiful, and her face looks rather darkish. She gnashes her teeth when her husband comes on her. Demons rule her, and she will deal with amulets (*Qame'oth*). But she fears God, and together with her husband they will perform good deeds. She will have sons and daughters from her husband, who will be rich and good. She will have milk and nurse her children herself. She will be haughty and sick at the ages of five, seven, and eleven; she will die at forty-one. She has a sign on her back.

[II] Male

For Gemini, see paragraph 32. He will have a sign on his face and body. He will go with great and thoughtful people, spend a lot of money and have none left. He will consider every man to be his friend and be hated for no reason. He will stay away from evil and his words will be heard. He will acquire many possessions and suffer for eight years. Many kindnesses will come to him from another woman, and he will find a house in a distant land. He will have a heartache and pain in his limbs, or in his right leg. Evil men will gossip against him, but they will fall in front of him. He will be the victim of others and be in danger. He will be punished and be beside himself. He will be sick at the ages of seven, twenty-five, and thirty-three. He will die at the age of eighty. He will have a sign on his hand, on his forehead, or on his thighs. He will be rich later in life and be affected in his eyes. He will be deceitful and haughty.

[Ⅱ] Female

She will be sick for five years and she is not that pretty. She is irritable and will marry twice. Her first husband will be poor, and so the second, but she will marry another man and live with him in good luck. She will be corpulent, speak a lot and be wise. She will endure seven miseries during her lifetime before she marries a third time. She will be sick at the ages of three [66], five, six, twelve, thirty-five, forty-six, and forty-eight. She will die at seventy. She has a sign on her breast, on her hands, or below.

[♋] Male

For Cancer, see paragraph 32. He will be subject to witchcraft and wander in distant lands. His heart will be inclined to evil and bad thoughts, and will want to transgress, however without doing it. He will be accepted among people. He will be sick at the age of three, or punished, or in danger, but then he will find much good. He will perform good deeds and feed others that are unknown to him, and many good things will occur to him. He will have one wife from whose star he will enjoy goodness. He will suffer from a bad reputation, and be very angry with his family. His end will be good, but he will suffer from his thighs, his knees, or one of his limbs. He will be sick at the age of eleven and die at eighty. He has a sign on his thighs.

[♋] Female

Her body will be nice and full. She will be modest with beautiful eyes and tall. At the age of one year and a half she will be sick. She will have many possessions but will endure troubles. She has a sign on her body, on her breasts, or on her belly. She will raise her relatives and help them. She will rejoice with women and not have a bad reputation in the world. She will suffer and constantly endure troubles from those who are jealous of her beauty and her wealth. Her relatives will give her a bad reputation, but her husband will love her as his own soul. She will be sick at the ages of three, five, thirty-five, forty-nine and sixty-four. She will die at eighty-four from consumption. She has signs on her breasts, on her belly, on her knees or on her head.

[♌] Male

For Leo, see paragraph 32. He will marry an important woman, but love her and hate her. He will always accumulate wealth and honor. His body is full and strong, and he speaks a lot with [67] much spirit. He will be wise, thinking well, and his words will be accepted. People will respect him, and he will love people. Yet, his friends will slander him, but without success. Many will eat at his table, and he will give everything away in time of trouble. A certain woman will cause him a bad reputation, but it is a lie. He raises orphans in his house and will suffer from one of his thighs or from his eyes later in life, but he will find a remedy. He is ready to sacrifice his life to save others from trouble. His end will be good, and he will see [the downfall of] his enemies. He will be sick at the ages of eighteen, thirty-eight, sixty-five, and die in his bed at eighty-five. He has a sign on his right thigh, on his hand, or on his foot.

[♌] Female

She is tall, modest and hairy. Her eyes are as pleasant as her skin. She will be receiving presents, but she will not rejoice and play with her friends. They will suspect her of wickedness, but she is clean from any evil. Her husband is jealous of her, and she suffers from it. And even her relatives constantly suspect her. She will give birth to sons in wealth and honor but will miscarry three times. She keeps herself from every bad thing, performs more good hidden deeds than her husband performs. If she lives to be forty-five years old, God will add to her honor. Her enemies will fall under her feet, and she will see their downfall. She will be sick at the ages of five, seven, twenty-six and thirty-five, and die at eighty. She has a sign on her hand, on her leg, on her finger, or on her face.

[♍] Male

For Virgo, see paragraph 32. He will marry one wife and live. His star shines in heaven, and he will live well and help the poor. He will take two wives, and see much good from the second one. He will be sick either from the cold or from the heat. He will have a bad reputation, but those that hate him will fall before him. He will suffer from one leg, or from the lower intestine, but will heal. He will live angrily with his family and be rebellious. He will be sick at the ages of thirteen, twenty-eight, and die at sixty. He has a sign on his genitals.

[68]

[♍] Female

She will be rich and give birth to sons. She has a sign on her body, on her face, or on her belly. Her face is reddish and she is haughty. Her thighs are thick and white. She will be dangerously sick at the age of three. People do not like her, but her deeds are clean, [although] she is suspected of wickedness. She bows down to everybody. Her star is good for wealth and sons but not for daughters. Her end is bad, and her star causes her to be sometimes dangerously sick. Evil spirits and demons will injure her at night. At the age of five, she will leave her house and return after two years. She loves her husband, but he does not love her and is jealous of her concerning other men. She will be sick at the ages of three, eight, nine, and sixteen, and she will die at thirty-seven. She has a sign on right leg and on her belly.

[♎] Male

For Libra, see paragraph 32. He will pursue charities and women. He has a sign on his body or on his foot. He shuns evil but does not have money. He will have one wife from whom he will have much good. He will move from his abode to another place or go to another neighborhood. Worthless people will give him a bad reputation. Enemies will rise against him, and he will fear them. He will be punished because of his sons or his brothers. He will be poor for two or three years and then find goodness and blessedness. He will take another wife and be rich with sons and daughters, and his words will be heard. He will suffer from the head, his arm or his eyes. He will be sick at the ages of eleven, thirty-one, and thirty-seven. If he recovers, he will die at eighty-one.

[♎] Female

She is nice looking and rich, and has a sign on her body. She is neither small nor tall. Her eyes are good. She will be sick at the age of six. She has to beware of anything hot and of dogs. Demons will trouble her in her youth, and she will be very sick but recover. There will be rumors that she rendered herself impure while married. She will control everything but suffer from her husband. She will perform *Mitzvot* and [69] acquire possessions. She will be respectable in her old age and die from a small worm. She will be sick at the ages of eleven, thirty-one, sixty-two, and die at seventy-two. She has a sign on her face, on her ribs, or on her left arm.

[♏] Male

For Scorpio, see paragraph 32. He will marry two women and help others. He has a sign on his chest, on his body, or on his shoulder. He will always look for bad and ugly things. He will be covetous, swear falsely, and be unhelpful. He will be ungrateful and always think about fraud. He will sell his possessions and be sick in his old age. He will go through a difficult period but later rise to greatness. He will be well for two years after his illness. He will have a lot of money and acquire fields and vineyards. He will be told many secrets and will not reveal them. He will be sick at the age of forty-seven, and if he recovers, he will live until eighty-six. He has a sign on his shoulders, on his thighs, on his eyes and his head. He will marry, find great wealth, and earn much.

[♏] Female

Her husband will suspect her of adultery, as she does whatever she desires. She has a sign on her face, on her shoulder, on her breasts, or on her thigh. She is very stingy. She will be sick at the age of eighteen months. She will be suspected of debauchery; she is a talker and is quarrelsome. She will marry a man of distinguished birth and have sons and daughters. She will be sick at the age of nine but will heal with amulets. She will have many sons; her relatives will rejoice with her, but she will live miserably. She will be sick at the ages of fifteen, eighteen, and thirty-four, and if she survives, she will live until sixty-four. She has a sign on her eyes, breasts and genitals, and on her left arm. She likes wine, oil, and honey.

[♐] Male

For Sagittarius, see paragraph 32. He will marry twice and go to distant lands. He has a sign on his hand, on his body, or on his face. He will befriend good people, and will pursue peace between [70] his fellowmen, and between man and his wife. His star shines in heaven. He respects people, but people do not respect him, and some will hate him. He will be sick at the age of eight years but will recover. Then, he will find much goodness and will walk with great people. Others desire to eat at his table and enjoy his possessions. He will have much money, and if witchcraft is worked against him, it is not because of his star. He will have sons, and others will be fed at his table. His enemies will bite him like dogs, and he will lose other people's money for no reason. He will take three wives and will have sons from the first one. He will have much money from the second one. The third one will be a virgin from whom he will have good sons, with the help of his star. He will bury his father and mother and be sick at the ages of seven, sixteen, nineteen, forty-eight, and die at seventy-eight. He has a sign on his hipbones. It will break twice, and thus he will walk slowly.

[✗] Female

She has a blemish on her body, a sign on her forehead, or on her foot. She will suffer from hemorrhoids and will be sick at the ages of three, six, sixteen, eighteen, twenty-six, thirty-eight, forty-five, and die at eighty. She will be an orphan at an early age and suck milk from many women, but not from her mother. She will be afraid of everything and will accumulate water in her belly. Later in life, she will be deranged and commit adultery; she will be bad for thirteen years. She is a talker and a liar. She tells her husband: "I do not love you". She has a sign on her shoulder.

[♑] Male

For Capricorn, see paragraph 32. He will have twin sons. He will be wise in all his ways, and live eighty years. He is inventive but has evil thoughts. He swears falsely and curses people a lot. He does not pray daily and does not speak in front of anyone wiser than he is. He walks proudly and will endure suffering for a while. Later, he will find goodness and repent from his bad deeds. He will marry twice. One is a widow who will live with him for thirteen years, and from whom he will have two sons. After her death, he will marry a virgin, from whom [71] he will have sons. His words are heard within his family. He rejoices the possessions of others. His relatives speak badly to injure him, but they will fall before him, and he will succeed in his endeavors. He will suffer from his loins, from his belly, or from his eyes. Others enjoy his money but are ungrateful. He is rebellious; his mind is restless, and he likes women. He will be sick at the ages of three, fifty, and die wealthy at eighty-four. He has a sign on his head or on his leg.

[♉] Female

She will be pretty, distrust her husband, and cause others to envy him. She likes sexual intercourse, and all will distrust her for no reason. Her star is bad, and she is suspected of theft. She will lose her mind in the future. She will have two sons and one daughter, but only one son and one daughter will be in her bed. She makes vows, and the evil eye rules her. At the end of her life, she will be going from place to place and not return to her house. She will be sick at the ages of three, eleven, nineteen, fifty-one and die at seventy-seven. She has a sign on her face, on her forehead, or on her left leg.

[♒] Male

For Aquarius, see paragraph 32. He will marry twice. He is nice looking, and has a sign on his body. He changes his mind easily but will not miss anything. He spends a lot and will be left with little money. He is well liked because of his favors. He knows business transactions well, pursues philanthropy and justice. He will have two wives and see goodness from the second one. He will have many possessions, and buy many more. His sons will hate him for no reason and will want to hurt him through sorcery. His family will slander him but to no avail, and they will fall on the ground before him. He does everything secretly and does not reveal anything to anyone; he keeps silent. He will be in great trouble but will be saved. He is jealous of others but will repent. He is not a craftsman and will suffer from a leg in old age. He will be sick at the ages of eleven and sixty-two, and will die wealthy at ninety-six. He has a sign on his loins, or in his eyes.

[72]

[♒] Female

She is a talker and she is pleasant. She will at times be rich or poor, but will have an income. She has a sign on her body: on her shoulder, on her face, or on her thigh. She makes a good impression on all those who see her. She is playful and has a pleasant voice. She gives to others when she gains for herself and shows that she is worthy. She does not commit any injustice. She shows love to her husband. She will be sick from the intestine for a few years, and it is recommended that she does not eat any neck, or beef meat at that time. She is well liked and holds her own opinion. Her star will be alternately full or empty. She will be sick at the ages of four, seventeen, nineteen, thirty-one, and will die at forty-four.

[)(] Male

For Pisces, see paragraph 32. He loves peace and people. He has a sign on his hips, on his belly, or on his thigh. He will father twins, either he or his father, his brothers or his own son. He has luck; merchandise will come to him, and nothing will be lacking in the house. He will stand by his word and hate evil. He is not afraid of illness and trouble. He is a good man who hates theft, robbery, slander and lies. He loves every man; yet, they do not love him but hate him for no reason. They plot evil things against him and slander him, but to no avail, for they will fall before him on the ground. He will find much goodness but will suffer for three years. He speaks and acts secretly. He will bury his wife and marry another one, whose star will be like his. He will live well with her, but she also will die. He will then marry other two women: a good one, and a bad one. One of them will give him a bad reputation. He will suffer from his eyes, from his loins, or from his head, but will heal. He will have a good name in his old age, and his end will be good. He will be sick at the ages of twelve and eighty-one, and die at eighty-five. He loves truth and hates lies.

[)(] Female

She will give birth in pain and sickness. Evil spirits will afflict her. She will be sick in her leg, in her head, and be orphaned at birth. She will suffer much from her belly. All her [73] prayers will be answered. She has a sign on her body, and she annoys her relatives. She will give birth to twins, and will be troubled by witchcraft. Demons will hurt her belly. She will suffer from her eyes, and she will not be able to stand in one place. Her husband will be among the choicest and nice, but she will soon bury him. If she remarries, she will not be happy with the second one who will hate her all the days of his life. She will have sons and daughters, but will suffer for a long time. She should not step out of her house at night. True slander will spread about her. She will be sick at the ages of three, seven, eleven, fourteen, twenty-five, twenty-eight, forty-four, sixty-two, and will die at eighty-two. She has a sign on her genitals, on her knees, and under her foot. Blessed be He who knows the secrets of men.

135

Your children have sons and daughters.	*Ayq* (איק)
Your children have sons and one daughter.	*Bkr* (בכר)
They have a son and a daughter.	*Glsh* (גלש)
They have sons and no daughter.	*Dmt* (דמת)
They have daughters and no sons.	*Hnk* (הנך)
They have one son.	*Vsm* (וסם)
They have one daughter.	*Z'an* (זען)
They have neither sons nor daughters.	*'hpp* (חפף)
The have no sons or daughters: they all died.	*Ttztz* (טצץ)

136

This medicine is very good for this patient.	*Avk'ashp* (אוכעשף)

It is good, but it contains a drug.   *Bzlpttz* (בזלפתץ)

It is not good for him, for it contains sicknesses. It is good for someone else.   *G'hmtzk* (גחמצך)

He should not take it, for it may kill him.   *Dtnqs* (דטנקס)

It is good for this patient, but he has no hope.   *Hysrn* (היסרן)

[74]

137

This girl is waiting for her mate; he is coming and will betroth her right away.   *Atpn* (אטפן)

She cannot be betrothed, for her mate is too young.   *Bytzp* (ביצף)

He is far away, but he will come and betroth her rapidly.   *Gkqtz* (גככץ)

He is not coming here; she has to go to him.   *Dlr* (דלר)

Her betrothal is prevented by witchcraft.   *Hmsh* (המש)

She will not be betrothed, for a demon wants her.   *Vnt* (ונת)

Her mate is married and will take her after his wife dies.   *Zsk* (זסך)

She has no mate, and she will die so.   *'h 'as* (חעס)

138

If you want to know which [*Mitzvah* you have to perform in order to heal an illness], arrange the six-hundred-thirteen *Mitzvot* in front of you according to Maimonides, cast the lots, and put together the letter of the first one with that of the second. Count the result over the six-hundred-thirteen *Mitzvot*. The *Mitzvah* on which it falls is the one you have to perform in order to heal.

139

If you want to know which day of the month is good for anything, see paragraph 115. That day is the good one.

140

This merchandise is good for you; buy it.	*Ahṭmpsh* (אהטמפש)
It bears a profit, but a small one.	*Bvyntztp* (בוינצתף)
It is impossible to profit from it; wait, and it will rise.	*Gzksqktz* (גזכסקדץ)
Do not buy it, for you will lose a lot.	*D'hl'arm* (דחלערם)

141

This house is propitious for having children.	*Adzym 'aqtn* (אדזימעעקתן)
[75] It will not prevent children.	*Bh'hknprkp* (בההחכנפרדף)
Do not go there; it is bad for children.	*Gvṭlstzshtz* (גוטלסצצששץ)

142

This object is not lost but kept.	*Avk'ashp* (אוכעעשף)
It is not lost; look for it, and you will find it in your house.	*Bzlpttz* (בזלפתץ)
Someone found it and will give it to you, but he is playing with it.	*G'hmtzk* (גחמצך)

An honest person found it; announce it, and he will return it.   *Dtnqs* (דטנקס)

A wicked man found it and will never return it.   *Hysrn* (היסרן)

143

If you go to the prince, your wish will be granted.   *Ahtmpshn* (אהטמפשן)

He will agree only partially to your request.   *Bvyntztp* (בוינצתף)

He will grant your wish if you pay.   *Gzksqktz* (גזכסקדץ)

You will not succeed with this request.   *D'hl'arm* (דחלערם)

144

That thing was stolen by the suspected one.   *Ahtmpshn* (אהטמפשן)

His wife stole it, and he does not know about it.   *Bvyntztp* (בוינצתף)

His son stole it, and he does not know about it.   *Gzksqktz* (גזכסקדץ)

His sons stole it, and he knows it.   *D'hl'arm* (דחלערם)

145

If you want to know which way to go and succeed, arrange the letters of the alphabet as follows: *A* ('א) in the east, *B* ('ב) in the south, *G* ('ג) in the west, *D* ('ד) in the north, and so on until the end of the twenty-seven letters. Then, cast the lot and go wherever it falls.

[76]

146

The new prince is a good person, and he will be good with you.   *Azmqn* (אזמקן)

He will do neither good nor evil.   *B'hnrp* (בחנרף)

He likes bribes and presents.   *Gtsshtz* (גטסשץ)

He is good, but his advisers are wicked; so, speak to him.   *Dy'at* (דיעת)

He is good but rich.   *Hkpk* (הכפך)

He is wicked, rich, and likes possessions.   *Vltzm* (ולצם)

147

Your *Neshamah* came only to learn *Kabbalah*.   *Avk'ashp* (אוכעשף)

It came to learn theology.   *Bzlpttz* (בזלפתץ)

It came to learn every type of *Kabbalah*.   *G'hmtzk* (גחמצך)

It came to learn Talmud and *Kabbalah*.   *Dtnqs* (דטנקס)

It came to learn Talmud, but not *Kabbalah*.   *Hysrn* (היסרן)

148

This woman is good for you for bringing wealth and children.   *Ayq* (איק)

She is good for wealth but not for children.   *Bkr* (בכר)

She is good for children but not for wealth.   *Glsh* (גלש)

She is average for wealth and children.	*Dmt* (דמת)
She is average for wealth and will give birth to girls.	*Hnk* (הנך)
She is good for wealth and will bring mainly boys.	*Vsm* (וסם)
She is bad for wealth and children.	*Z'an* (זען)
Do not desire this woman, for she will cause your death.	*'hpp* (חפף)
She is good for wealth and will bring boys.	*Ṯtztz* (טצץ)

149

Your father is alive and well.	*Aḥtmpshn* (אהטמפשן)
He is sick, but will recover.	*Bvyntztp* (בוינצתף)
[77] He is sick and almost dead.	*Gzksqktz* (גזכסקקץ)
He is already dead.	*D'hl'arm* (דחלערם)

150

Your wife is not giving birth because of you.	*Aḥtmpshn* (אהטמפשן)
She is preventing it.	*Bvyntztp* (בוינצתף)
If she takes medicine, she will give birth.	*Gzksqktz* (גזכסקקץ)
This man is struck by demons. He needs an amulet and he will bear children.	*D'hl'arm* (דחלערם)

151

If you want to know which month the theft was made, cast two lots and unite them. Divide the outcome according to the months of the year, whether it is a regular or a leap year. And wherever the number falls, etc. .

152

This merchandise is not stolen; take it without fear.	*Adzym'aqtn* (אדזימעקתן)
Do not worry, even though it is stolen; no one will claim it.	*Bh'hknprkp* (בההחכנפרדף)
This merchandise is stolen. Do not take it; perhaps it will be found in your possession.	*Gvṭlstzshstz* (גוטלסצששסץ)

153

There is a great precious thing in this house.	*Aḥṭmpshn* (אהטמפשן)
It has a fine precious thing.	*Bvyntztp* (בוינצתף)
It has some money.	*Gzksqktz* (גזכסקקדץ)
It has nothing, so do not bother.	*D'hl'arm* (דחלערם)

154

The precious thing is in the eastern wall.	*Avk'ashp* (אוכעשף)
It is in the southern wall.	*Bzlpttz* (בזלפתץ)
[78] It is in the western wall.	*G'hmtzk* (גחמצך)
It is the northern wall.	*Dṭnqs* (דטנקס)

It is under the ground in the house.   *Hysrn* (היסרן)

155

If you want to know where in the ground of the house the precious thing is hidden, divide it crosswise in four parts. Call the southeast corner east, the southwest corner south, the northwest corner west, and the northeast corner north. Then, stand in the center with a clean body, dressed in white clean clothing, on a certain day, at a certain hour, and say the prayer mentioned in the introduction. Then, start with the lots, and put together the letter of the first lot with that of the second one. Divide the outcome according to the four corners. Go east, south, west, and north, and continue until you finish. Divide the final spot crosswise as mentioned above, and also pray as above. This is a new lot. The treasure is at the spot where you finish this round. You can go on like this until you stand on the very spot of the precious thing itself. So shall you proceed, unless it is in the wall. This is enough for those who understand. Be successful.

156

If you want to know if it is deeply buried or not, I will arrange these letters and their measurements for you:

These letters measure a hand-breath.   *Ahṭmpshn* (אהטמפשן)

These letters measure a span, which are three hand-breaths.   *Bvyntztp* (בוינצתף)

These letters measure a cubit, which are three spans.   *Gzksqktz* (גזכסקךץ)

[79] These letters measure a man's height, which is three cubits.   *D'hl'arm* (דחלערם)

I inform you now that the *Alef* of *Ahṭmpsh"n* measures one hand-breath, *He*, the second letter, two hand-breaths, *Teth*, the third letter, three hand-breaths, *Daleth*, the fourth letter, four hand-breaths, *Peh*, the fifth letter, five hand-breaths, *Shin* six hand-breaths, and *Nun* seven hand-breaths. This method applies also for the spans, the cubits, and man's height. Once you know the measurements, cast the lots, and see the results of the first and second ones. For instance, if the first lot is *Teth* whose measurement is three hand-breaths, and the second is *Yod* whose measurement is three spans, the treasure is buried three spans and three hand-breaths deep. If the second lot is *Kaf*, then it is buried three cubits and three hand-breaths deep. This is the method: you have to add up the results of the first and second lots, and you shall know the depth. However, if the first lot is a hand-breath, a span, a cubit or a man's height, and the second one is identical, it means that the depth is as shown by the first letter. The rule is that if the letters are identical, you go by the first lot.

157

This treasure is not enchanted and you will get it.

Aghztkmspshkntz (אגהזטכמספקשדזץ)

It is enchanted, and you will not be able to get it.

Bdv'hyn 'aptzrtsp (בדוחילנעפצרתסף)

158

Play dice and win.

Ahtmpshn (אהטמפשן)

If you play today, you will win.

Bvyntztp (בוינצתף)

You will not win against this man.

Gzksqktz (גזכסקדץ)

Do not play; you do not have any luck.

D'hl'arm (דחלערם)

159

The trustee did not transgress against the deposit.

Avk'ashp (אוכעשף)

He thought of transgressing against it.   *Bzlpttz* (בזלפתץ)

[80] He did not transgress, but his family wanted to.   *G'hmtzk* (גחמצך)

He did not transgress, but his family did.   *Dṭnqs* (דטנקס)

He transgressed against the deposit.   *Hysrn* (היסרן)

160

Learn this trade and profit from it.   *Ahṭmpshn* (אהטמפשן)

You may learn it, but you do not need it for your subsistence.   *Bvyntztp* (בוינצתף)

Do not bother to learn it; you will not have any luck with it.   *Gzksqktz* (גזכסקךץ)

Do not learn it; it will only damage you.   *D'hl'arm* (דחלערם)

161

This slave went free.   *Avk'ashp* (אוכעשף)

He did not yet go free, but he found the money for it.   *Bzlpttz* (בזלפתץ)

He will not go free until he finds the money for it.   *G'hmtzk* (גחמצך)

He will escape, for he does not have money.   *Dṭnqs* (דטנקס)

He will die as a prisoner.   *Hysrn* (היסרן)

162

If you want to know about the thief's appearance, arrange all these in front of you.

First part

(1) His eyes and beard are dark, his body is tall; (2) as mentioned, his body is average; (3) as mentioned, his body is short; (4) his eyes are dark; his body is tall; his beard is chestnut; (5) as mentioned, his body is average; (6) as mentioned, his body is short; (7) his eyes are dark; his beard is reddish and his body is tall; (8) as mentioned, his body is average; (9) as mentioned, his body is short; (10) his eyes are reddish; his beard chestnut; his body is tall; (11) as mentioned, his body is average; (12) as mentioned, his body is short; (13) his eyes and beard are reddish, and his body is long; (14) [81] as mentioned. his body is average; (15) as mentioned, his body is short; (16) his eyes are reddish; his beard is yellow; his body is long; (17) as mentioned, his body is average; (18) as mentioned, his body is short; (19) his eyes are green; his beard is chestnut; his body is tall; (20) as mentioned, his body is average; (21) as mentioned, his body is short; (22) his eyes are green; his beard is chestnut; his body is tall; (23) as mentioned, his body is average; (24) as mentioned, his body is short; (25) his eyes are green; his beard is chestnut; his body is tall; (26) as mentioned, his body is average; (27) as mentioned, his body is short; (28) his eyes are blue; his beard chestnut; his body is tall; (29) as mentioned, his body is average; (30) as mentioned, his body is short; (31) his eyes are as mentioned; his beard is reddish; his body is tall; (32) as mentioned, his body is average; (33) as mentioned, his body is short; (34) his eyes are as mentioned; his beard is yellow; his body is tall; (35) as mentioned, his body is average; (36) as mentioned, his body is short.

Second part

(37) His eyes are dark; he is thin-bearded; his body is tall; (38) as mentioned, his body is average; (39) as mentioned, his body is short; (40) his eyes are as mentioned; he has a thin reddish beard; his body is tall; (41) as mentioned, his body is average; (42) as mentioned, his body is short; (43) his eyes are as mentioned; he

has a thin chestnut beard; his body is tall; (44) as mentioned. his body is average; (45) as mentioned, his body is short; (46) his eyes are as mentioned; he has a thin reddish beard; his body is tall; (47) as mentioned, his body is average; (48) as mentioned, his body is short; (49) his eyes are as mentioned; he has a thin yellow beard; his body is tall; (50) as mentioned, his body is average; (51) as mentioned, his body is short; (52) his eyes are green; he has a thin chestnut beard; his body is tall; (53) as mentioned, his body is average; (54) as mentioned, his body is short; (55) his eyes look like doves; he has a thin reddish beard; his body is tall; (56) as mentioned, his body is average; (57) as mentioned, his body is short; (58) his eyes look like doves; he has a thin yellow beard; his body is tall; (59) as mentioned, his body is average; (60) as mentioned, his body is short; (61) his eyes are blue; his beard is chestnut; his body is tall; (62) as mentioned, his body is average; (63) as mentioned, his body is short; (64) his eyes are as mentioned; he has a thin reddish beard; his body is tall; (65) as mentioned, his body is average; (66) as mentioned, [82] his body is short; (67) his eyes are as mentioned; he has a thin yellow beard; his body is tall; (68) as mentioned, his body is average; (69) as mentioned, his body is short.

Third part

(70) His beard is dark; his ears large; the nose and the mouth are average; (71) as mentioned, his eyes stand out; the ears and the mouth are average; (72) his beard is as mentioned; the nose is large; the ears, the eyes and the mouth are average; (73) as mentioned, his mouth is large; the ears, the nose and the eyes are average; (74) as mentioned, the ears and the eyes are large; the nose and the mouth are average; (75) as mentioned, the ears and the nose are large; the eyes and the mouth are average; (76) as mentioned, the nose and the mouth are large; the eyes and the nose are average; (77) as mentioned, the eyes stand out; the nose is large; the ears and the mouth are average; (78) as mentioned, his eyes stand out; the mouth is large; the ears and the nose are average; (79) as mentioned, the nose and the mouth are large; the ears and the eyes are average; (80) as mentioned, the eyes stand

out; the ears and the nose are large; the mouth is average; (81) as mentioned, the ears, the nose and the mouth are large; the eyes are average; (82) as mentioned, the eyes stand out; the nose and the mouth are large; the ears are average; (83) as mentioned, his eyes stand out; the ears and the mouth are large; the nose is average; (84) as mentioned, the eyes stand out; the ears, the nose and the mouth are large; (85) his beard is chestnut; his ears are large; the nose, the eyes and the mouth are average; (86) as mentioned, his eyes stand out; the ears, the nose and the mouth are average; (87) as mentioned, the nose is large; the ears, the eyes and mouth are average; (88) as mentioned, the mouth is large; the ears, the eyes and the nose are average; (89) as mentioned, the eyes stand out; the ears are large; the nose and the mouth are average; (90) as mentioned, the ears and the nose are large; the eyes and the mouth are average; (91) as mentioned, the ears and the mouth are large; the eyes and the nose are average; (92) as mentioned, the eyes stand out; the nose is large; the ears and the mouth are average; (93) as mentioned, the eyes stand out; the mouth is large; the ears and the nose are average; (94) as mentioned, the mouth is large; the ears and the eyes are average; (95) as mentioned, the ears and the nose are large; the mouth is average; (96) as mentioned, the eyes, the ears and the mouth are large; the nose is average; (97) as mentioned, the ears, the nose and the mouth are large; the eyes are average; (98) as mentioned, the eyes stand out; the nose and the mouth are large; the ears are average; (99) as mentioned, the ears, the nose and the mouth are large; (100) his beard is reddish; his ears are large; the eyes, the nose and the mouth are average; (101) as mentioned, the eyes stand out; the ears and the mouth are average; (102) as mentioned, the nose is large; the ears [83], the mouth and the eyes are average; (103) as mentioned, the mouth is large; the ears, the nose and the eyes are average; (104) as mentioned, the eyes stand out; the ears are large; the mouth and the nose are average; (105) as mentioned, the ears and the nose are large; the eyes and the mouth are average; (106) as mentioned, the ears and the mouth are large; the nose and the eyes are average; (107) as mentioned, his eyes stand out; the nose is large; the ears and the mouth are average; (108) as mentioned, the ears and the mouth are large; the eyes and the nose are average; (109) as mentioned, the nose and the mouth are large; the ears and the eyes are average; (110) as mentioned, the eyes stand out; the ears and the nose are large; the mouth is average; (111) as mentioned, the ears and the mouth are large; the nose is average; (112) as mentioned, the ears, the nose and the mouth are large; the eyes are average; (113) his eyes stand out; the nose and the mouth are large; the ears are average; (114) as mentioned, his eyes stand out; the ears, the nose and the mouth are large; (115) his beard is yellow; the ears are large; the eyes, the nose and the mouth are average; (116) as mentioned, his eyes stand out; the ears, the nose and the mouth are average; (117) as mentioned, the nose is large; the eyes, the mouth and the ears are average; (118) as mentioned, the mouth is large; the eyes, the nose and the ears are average; (119) as mentioned, his eyes stand out; the ears are large; the mouth and the nose are average; (120) as mentioned, the ears and the nose are large; the eyes and the mouth are average; (121) as mentioned, the ears and the mouth are large; the eyes and the nose are average; (122) as mentioned, his eyes stand out; the nose is large; the ears and the mouth are average; (123) as mentioned, the mouth is large; the ears and the nose are average; (124) as mentioned, the nose and the mouth are large; the ears and the eyes are average; (125) as mentioned, his eyes stand out; the ears and the nose are large; the mouth is average; (126) as mentioned the ears and the mouth are large, the nose is average (127) as mentioned, the ears, the nose and the mouth are large; the eyes are average; (128) as mentioned, his eyes stand out; the nose and the mouth are large; the ears are average; (129) as mentioned, the ears, the nose and the mouth are large.

Fourth part

(130) His beard is dark; his right eye is blind; (131) as mentioned, his left eye is blind; (132) as mentioned, his nose is mutilated; (133) as mentioned, his right arm is mutilated; (134) as mentioned, his left arm is mutilated; (135) as mentioned, his right leg is mutilated; (136) as mentioned, his left leg is mutilated; (137) his right eye is blind and his right arm mutilated; (138) as mentioned, his right eye is blind and his left arm mutilated; (139) as mentioned, his left eye is blind and his left arm mutilated; (140) as mentioned, his left eye

is blind and his right arm mutilated; (141) as mentioned, [84] his right eye is blind and his right leg mutilated; (142) as mentioned, his right leg is mutilated; (143) as mentioned, his left eye is blind and his left leg mutilated; (144) as mentioned, his right leg is mutilated; (145) his beard is reddish and his right eye is blind; (146) as mentioned, his left eye is blind; (147) as mentioned, his nose is mutilated; (148) as mentioned, his right arm is mutilated; (149) as mentioned, his left arm is mutilated; (150) as mentioned, his right leg is mutilated; (151) as mentioned, his left leg is mutilated; (152) as mentioned, his right eye is blind; his right hand is mutilated; (153) as mentioned, his right eye is blind; his left hand is mutilated; (154) as mentioned, his left eye is blind; his right hand is mutilated; (155) as mentioned, his left eye is blind; his left hand is mutilated; (156) as mentioned, his right eye is blind; his left leg is mutilated; (157) as mentioned, his left eye is blind; his left leg is mutilated; (158) as mentioned, his right eye is mutilated; his left leg is mutilated; (159) as mentioned, his left eye is mutilated; his right leg is mutilated; (160) as mentioned, his beard is chestnut; his right eye is mutilated; (161) as mentioned, his left eye is mutilated; (162) as mentioned, his nose is mutilated; (163) as mentioned, his right arm is mutilated; (164) as mentioned, his left arm is mutilated; (165) as mentioned, his right leg is mutilated; (166) as mentioned, his left leg is mutilated; (167) as mentioned, his right eye is blind and his right arm is mutilated; (168) as mentioned, his right eye is blind and his left arm is mutilated; (169) as mentioned, his left eye is blind and his right arm is mutilated; (170) as mentioned, his left eye is blind and his left arm is mutilated; (171) as mentioned, his right eye is blind and his right leg is mutilated; (172) as mentioned, his right eye is blind and his left leg is mutilated; (173) his beard is yellow; his right eye is blind; (174) as mentioned, his left eye is blind, (175) as mentioned, his nose is mutilated; (176) as mentioned, his right arm is mutilated; (177) as mentioned, his left arm is mutilated; (178) as mentioned, his right leg is mutilated; (179) as mentioned, his left leg is mutilated; (180) as mentioned, his right eye is blind and his right arm is mutilated; (181) as mentioned, his left arm is mutilated; (182) as mentioned, his left eye is blind and his left leg is mutilated; (183) as mentioned, his left eye is blind and his right leg is mutilated; (184) as mentioned, his left eye is blind and his right arm mutilated; (185) as mentioned, his left eye is blind; his left arm is mutilated; (186) as mentioned, his right eye is blind and his right leg is mutilated; (187) as mentioned, his right eye is blind and his left leg is mutilated; (188) as mentioned, his right hand has six fingers; (189) as mentioned, his left hand has six fingers; (190) as mentioned, his left foot has six toes; (191) as mentioned, his left [85] foot has six toes; (192) as mentioned, both his hands have six fingers; (193) as mentioned, both his feet have six toes; (194) as mentioned, his hands and feet have six fingers; (195) as mentioned, he has humps on his back; (196) as mentioned, he has humps in front and on the back. This is the end of all the looks. Praise to God who formed the luminaries.

Now that you know from the lot that the thief has a beard, cast a lot. Divide the alphabet into four parts, and in whichever part it falls, here is the look of the thief.

Now that you know which part, cast the lot again. Put together the letter of the first lot with the second, divide the result on the four parts, and wherever that number falls is the thief's appearance.

This is the method to follow if you want to know how to open the treasure: just repeat the thief's method.

163

You can be sure that this mission will earn you a lot of money.	*Avk'ashp* (אוכעשף)
You will not earn so much money.	*Bzlpttz* (בזלפתץ)
Some will harass you, so you will earn little money.	*G'hmtzk* (גחמצך)
You will earn a lot, but it will be stolen on the road.	*Dtnqs* (דטנקס)
Everything will be stolen from you.	*Hysrn* (היסרן)

164

This prince will not rule for more than a year.   *Adzy'aqtn* (אדזימעקתן)

He will not even rule for three years.   *Bh'hknprqp* (בההכנ
פרקף)

He will last until the sabbatical year.   *Gv̱tlktzsshstz*
(גוטלכצסששסץ)

If you want to know how many weeks, months or years one will rule, cast the lot, and put together the first with the second letter. Divide the result according to the number of weeks, months of that year, or years of that sabbatical cycle. Wherever the number falls is the number of weeks, months, or years of that ruler.

[86]

165

Have confidence in your *Kabbalah* learning, for you are not responsible.   *Aḥtpmshn* (אהטמפשן)

If you want to learn it in depth, take a teacher; do not make a mistake, and you will be responsible.   *Bvyntztp* (בוינצתף)

If you want to lean *Kabbalah* in depth, follow this rule: In my flesh I shall see God.   *Gzkqktz* (גזכסקדץ)

Do not learn it; your mind cannot take it, and you will err.   *D'hl'ars* (דחלערם)

166

If you are sailing and you want to know how long you will be at sea, divide the alphabet into three parts as follows. If the first lot comes out for the days, put it together with the letter of the second lot, and divide it according to the days of the month. Wherever the number ends is the number of days (*Adzym 'aqtn*) of your sailing. So is the method for the weeks (*Bh'hknprkp*). If the first lot comes out for the weeks, or for the months (*Gvtlstzshstz*), take again the letter of the second lot and unite them. Divide them according to the weeks or the months, and wherever the count ends, this is the time of your sailing.

167

This woman is your mate.	*Ahmpshn* (אהמפשן)
She is not your mate, but she will be in the future.	*Bvyntztp* (בוינצתף)
She is your mate, but because of your sins, you cannot take her.	*Gdksqkp* (גדכסקדץ)
She is not your mate; do not take her.	*D'hl'arm* (דחלערם)

168

This theft will be found; it is being sold.	*Avk'ashp* (אוכעשף)
Part will be found, and then the rest of it too.	*Bzlpttz* (בזלפתץ)
[87] Only part will be found, but not the rest of it.	*G'hmtzk* (גחמצך)
You will only find one part of it.	*Dtnqs* (דטנקס)
You will not find it at all.	*Hysm* (היסרן)

169

Sow your grain and you will profit.	*Adzym 'aqtn* (אדזימעעקתן)

Sow it when the time is propitious.	*Bh'hknprkp* (בההחכנפרדף)
Do not sow it, for you will not profit at all.	*Gvṭlstzshstz* (גוטלסצששסץ)

170

Your brothers are well.	*A'hst* (אחסת)
One of them died.	*Dktzn* (דכצן)
They are all well, but one is sick.	*Bṯ'ak* (בטעך)
Both your brothers died.	*Hlqp* (הלקף)
One is well, but the rest are sick.	*Gyps* (גיפם)
Only one brother lives.	*Vmrtz* (ומרץ)
None of them survived; only their children are alive.	*Znsh* (זנש)

171

This is a good trade; it will make you a lot of profit.	*Avk'ashp* (אוכעשף)
It is a good emergency trade that will earn just enough.	*Bzlpttz* (בזלפתץ)
Do not make that trade your main one, but have another one.	*G'hmtzk* (גחמצך)
Do not refrain from this trade; otherwise, you will be pressed.	*Dṯnqs* (דטנקס)
Do not engage in it, for it will damage you.	*Hysrn* (היסרן)

172

This suspicion is false.	*Aḥtmpshn* (אהטמפשן)
It is false, but what he is not suspected of is true.	*Bvntztp* (בוינצתף)
[88] He started to do what he is suspected of, but he did not finish.	*Gzksqktz* (גזכסקדץ)
Whatever he is suspected of is true.	*D'hl'arm* (דחלערם)

173

Go on this mission; you will come back healthy and with your possessions.	*Aḥtmpshn* (אהטמפשן)
You will come back healthy, but not with your possessions.	*Bvyntztp* (בוינצתף)
You will come back with your possessions, but you will be sick.	*Gzksqktz* (גזכסקדץ)
You will not come back in peace.	*D'hl'arm* (דחלערם)

174

The vice regent has been replaced. The first one died; this one came instead.	*Adzym'aqtn* (אדזימעקתן)
He has not yet been replaced, but they want to do so.	*Knprkpbh'h* (בהחכנפרדף)
He has not been replaced and will not be replaced.	*Gvtstzshtz* (גוטסצששץ)

175

The hatred comes because she is not his	*Aḥtmpshn* (אהטמפשן)

mate.

It comes because of enemies who incite fighting between them.
   Bvyntztp (בוינצתף)

It is because of a demon that plays with her.
   Gzksqktz (גזכסקדץ)

It comes because of witchcraft.
   D'hl'arm (דחלערם)

176

This woman is pregnant.
   Ḥtmpshn (הטמפשן)

She is not pregnant, but her period is late.
   Bvntztp (בוינצתף)

She is not pregnant, but her period has ceased.
   Gzksqktz (גזכסקדץ)

She is pregnant, but the fetus died inside her.
   D'hl'arm (דחלערם)

177

Be assured that she will deliver soon without any harm.
   Avk'ashp (אוכעשף)

She will suffer during delivery, but she will be saved.
   Bzlpttz (בזלפתץ)

[89] She will suffer much, but she will be saved.
   G'hmtzk (גחמצך)

She will have a fast delivery, but she will not be saved.
   Dṭnks (דטנקס)

She will have a difficult delivery, but she will not be saved.
   Hysrn (היסרן)

178

You father is already on his way.	*Ahtmpshn* (אהטמפשן)
He wants to come; he is on the verge of travel.	*Bvyntztp* (בוינצתף)
He did not leave yet, but he will soon arrive.	*Gzksqktz* (גזכסקדץ)
He does not wish to come.	*D'hl'arm* (דחלערם)

179

This betrothal was not completed, for she is not his mate.	*Adzm 'aqtn* (אדזימעקתן)
It was not completed, but it will be in the future.	*Bh'hknprkp* (בההחכנפרדף)
It was not completed, but it will because of witchcraft.	*Gvtlstzshstz* (גוטלסצששסץ)

180

If you want to know whether someone has already left his place or not, see the answers in paragraph 178.

181

Request the theft from the thief, and he will return it.	*Adzym 'aqtn* (אדזימעקתן)
Request it only through a relative.	*Bh'hknprkp* (בההחכנפרדף)
Do not bother, for he will not return anything.	*Gvtlstzshstz* (גוטלסצששסץ)

182

Dig for the treasure and do not worry, for he does not know.   *Aḥtmpshn* (אהטמפשן)

Do not tell your wife, for he will know through her.   *Bvyntztp* (בוינצתף)

[90] Keep it from your family, for they will reveal it.   *Gzksqtz* (גזכסקץ)

Do not look for the treasure; it is not good for you.   *D'hl'arm* (דחלערם)

183

If you want to know which day of the week to sow the seed and succeed, combine the letter of the first lot with that of the second one. Divide the result according to the days of the week, and wherever the final count falls on is the right day for sowing the seed. Alternatively, you can follow the method mentioned in paragraph 80.

184

Your brothers have boys and girls.   *Azmqn* (אזמקן)

They have boys and one girl.   *B'hnrp* (בחנרף)

They have boys, but no girls.   *Gtsshtz* (גטססשץ)

They have only one son.   *Dy'at* (דיעת)

They only have one daughter.   *Hkpk* (הכפך)

They do not have either boys or girls.   *Vltzm* (ולצם)

185

If you want to know which trade you should occupy yourself with in order to profit, write down all the trades you know, take the letters of the first and of the second lots, combine them, and divide the result according to the number of trades. Wherever the count ends is the trade you should choose.

186

Take that animal; you will succeed with it.	*Avk'ashp* (אוכעשף)
If you take it, watch it, for it will be stolen from you.	*Bzlpttz* (בזלפתץ)
If you take and you need it, do not keep it too long.	*G'hmtzk* (גחמצך)
[91] Do not take it, for it is stolen; it will be recognized and taken away.	*Dṭnqs* (דטנקס)
Do not take it, for it will quickly die.	*Hysrn* (היסרן)

187

If you want to know whether a suspect is one of those [written] in front of you, combine the letters of the first and second lots, divide the result according to their number. Start from the right side, and wherever the count ends is your suspect.

188

The messenger is alive and well.	*Ayq* (איק)
He is sick but will recover.	*Bkr* (בכר)
He is sick and will not recover.	*Glsh* (גלש)

He is already dead.	*Dmt* (דמת)
He was killed on the way.	*Hnk* (הנך)
He drowned in the sea.	*Vsm* (וסם)
He was taken prisoner.	*Z'an* (זען)
He apostatized in custody; he will escape and come back.	*'hpp* (חפף)
He apostatized willingly, and he will not come back.	*Ttztz* (תצץ)

189

It is untrue that this woman is a suspect.	*Ahtmpshn* (אההטמפשן)
It is both true and untrue that she is a suspect.	*Bvyntztp* (בוינצתף)
She is not responsible.	*Gzksqktz* (גזכסקדץ)
It is true that she is a suspect.	*D'hl'arm* (דחלערם)

190

This woman dislikes her husband, for she is interested in someone else.	*Ahtmpshn* (אההטמפשן)
She dislikes him, for he is an adulterer.	*Bvyntztp* (בוינצתף)
[92] She dislikes him, for she is not his mate.	*Gzksqktz* (גזכסקדץ)
She dislikes him, for she is under a spell.	*D'hl'arm* (דחלערם)

191

Do not worry; this patient will soon rise	*Ahtmpshn* (אההטמפשן)

up.

He will be sick for a long time, but he will heal.   *Bvntztp* (בוינצתף)

He will heal from this illness, but he will get sick again and die.   *Gzksqktz* (גזכסקקדץ)

He is destined to die.   *D'hlarm* (דחלערם)

192

The baby was born under a good star, with happiness and life.   *Avṯnqs* (אוטנקס)

He was born under a good star, with happiness, but not for life.   *Bzysrn* (בזיסרן)

He was born for life but not for happiness.   *G'hkk'ashp* (גחכעשף)

He is average, neither good nor bad.   *Dlpttz* (דלפתץ)

He is bad for happiness and life.   *Hmtzk* (המצך)

193

Your son is alive and well.   *Ahṯmpshn* (אהטמפשן)

Your son is sick, but he will heal.   *Bvntztp* (בוינצתף)

Your son is sick and ready to die.   *Gzksqktz* (גזכסקקדץ)

Your son is already dead.   *D'hl'arm* (דחלערם)

194

Travel, even alone, for there is no Satan or evil.   *Ahṯmtshn* (אהטמפשן)

Do not travel alone, but only with a caravan.   *Bvyntztp* (בוינצתף)

Do not go even with a caravan, for you will lose your money.   *Gksqktz* (גזכסקדץ)

Do not go even with a caravan, for you will be killed.   *Dhl'arm* (דחלערם)

[93]

195

Do not worry; this man thinks of coming back.   *Avk'ashp* (אוכעשף)

He will tarry a lot, but he will come back.   *Bzlpttz* (בזלפתץ)

He will not come, for he ran away.   *G'hmtzk* (גחמצך)

He will not come, for he got married somewhere else.   *Dtnqs* (דטנקס)

He is already dead.   *Hysrn* (היסרן)

196

You will find this lost object in your house.   *Avk'ashp* (אוכעשף)

It will be found in another house.   *Bzlpttz* (בזלפתץ)

It will return to its original place, and it will be found there.   *G'hmtzk* (גחמצך)

A trusty man, who will return it to you, found it.   *Dtnqs* (דטנקס)

It was found by someone who left; you will not recover it.   *Hysrn* (היסרן)

197

Nothing will be left of this merchandise; you will gain from it.	*Adzym 'aqtn* (אדזימעקתן)
This merchandise will neither rise nor devalue.	*Bh'hknprkp* (בההחכנפרדף)
Sell it quickly, for it will devalue.	*Gvṭlstzshtz* (גוטלסצששסץ)

198

Do whatever you wanted; you will succeed.	*Adzym 'aqtn* (אדזימעקתן)
Nothing wrong will happen if you do it.	*Bh'hknprkp* (בההחכנפרדף)
Do not do it, something very bad will happen to you.	*Gvṭlstzshtz* (גוטלסצששץ)

199

If you want to know when to sow your seed and profit, put together the first and the second letter of the lots, divide the result according to the twelve hours of the day, and wherever the count ends is the hour for success.

[94]

200

If you want to know if your brothers will have boys or girls, do what is said in paragraph 184.

201

This rented house is good for you.	*Adzym 'aqtn* (אדזימעקתן)
You can rent it if you want.	*Bh'hknprkp* (בההחכנפרדף)
Do not rent this house; it is bad for you.	*Gvṭlstzshstz* (גוטלסצזששסץ)

202

Buy this field and you will profit.	*Ahṭmpshn* (אהטמפשן)
There are some contestants, so hold on to your deed.	*Bvyntztp* (בוינצתף)
You can buy it, if you wish.	*Gzksqktz* (גזכסקדץ)
Do not buy it; it is very bad for you.	*D'hl'arm* (דחלערם)

203

The messenger is nearing the city; he will be here soon.	*Ahṭmpshn* (אהטמפשן)
He is far away, but he is coming back.	*Bvyntztp* (בוינצתף)
He is still walking, but he will return.	*Gzksqktz* (גזכסקדץ)
He is far away, and he does not intend to return.	*D'hl'arm* (דחלערם)

204

This man hates so and so for no reason.	*Avk'ashp* (אוכעעשף)
He hates him, for he desires his wife.	*Bzlpttz* (בזלפתץ)

He hates him, for he saw him stealing.   *G'hmtzk* (גחמצך)

He hates him, for he caused harm between them.   *Dṯnqs* (דטנקס)

He hates so and so, because of the witchcraft that was done to them.   *Hysrn* (היסרן)

[95]

205

Your whole family is well.   *A'hst* (אחסת)

One son died, but the rest are well.   *Bṯ'ak* (בטעך)

Two of them died, but the rest are well.   *Gypm* (גיפם)

One son and one daughter died, and the rest are well.   *Dktzn* (דכצן)

One daughter died, and the rest are well.   *Hlqp* (הלקף)

You wife died, and the rest are well.   *Vmrtz* (ומרץ)

Your wife and one son died, but the others are well.   *Znsh* (זנש)

206

If you want to know how many years this newborn will live, put together the letters from the first and second lots, divide the result according to seventy-one. Wherever the count ends will be the years of his life. If it reaches seventy-one, he will live more than seventy years.

207

So and so loves you more than you love him.   *Ahṯmpshn* (אהטמפשן)

He loves you as much as you love him.   *Bvyntztp* (בוינצתף)

You love him and he does not hate you.   *Gzksqktz* (גזכסקדץ)

So and so hates you a lot.   *D'hl'arm* (דחלערם)

208

This lost object was found by a Jew.   *Avk'ashp* (אוכעשף)

It was found by an Arab.   *Bzlpttz* (בזלפתץ)

It was found by a Gentile.   *G'hmtzk* (גחמצך)

It was found by your son.   *Dṯnqs* (דטנקס)

It was found by your grandson.   *Hysrn* (היסרן)

[96]

209

The vine will give its fruit.   *Ahṯmpshtn* (אהטמפשן)

It will not give its fruit, but wine will be cheap.   *Bvyntztp* (בוינצתף)

It will give its fruit, but wine will be expensive.   *Gzksqktz* (גזכסקדץ)

It will not give its fruit, and wine will be expensive.   *D'hl'arm* (דחלערם)

210

It is good to learn the wisdom of so and so.   *Ahṯmpsh* (אהטמפש)

If you want to learn it, do it constantly.   *Bvyntztp* (בוינצתף)

It is very difficult, and you will not be able to learn it.   *Gzksqktz* (גזכסקדץ)

Do not learn it; it will harm you and you   *D'hl'arm* (דחלערם)
will not succeed.

211

If you want to know which day of the month to sow the seeds, put
together the letters of the first and second lots, divide the result
according to the days of the month, whether it is full or lacking, and
wherever the count ends is the day you will succeed.

212

He who goes out to war will win.   *Ahṯmpshn* (אהטמפשן)

He will not win or be vanquished.   *Bvyntztp* (בוינצתף)

They will make peace and not wage war.   *Gzksqktz* (גזכסקדץ)

He who goes out to war will be   *D'hl'arm* (דחלערם)
vanquished.

213

If you leave this town you will not find a   *Ahṯmpshn* (אהטמפשן)
better one.

It will be good for wealth, but not for   *Bvyntztp* (בוינצתף)
children.

[97] It will be good for children, but not   *Gzksqktz* (גזכסקדץ)
for wealth.

Leave this town, for it is bad for you.   *D'hl'arm* (דחלערם)

214

Take this slave; he is faithful and good   *Ahṯmpshn* (אהטמפשן)

for you.

He is good for you, but he is not faithful and will escape.	*Bvyntztp* (בוינצתף)
Do not take him, for he is no good.	*Gzksqktz* (גזכסקדץ)
Do not take him, for he will soon die.	*D'hl'arm* (דחלערם)

215

If you want to know how many thieves there were, take the letter of the first lot. If it is a unit, and the letter of the second lot is also a unit, divide the result in nine parts, and wherever the count ends — between one and nine — is the number of thieves. If the letter of the first lot is three, and the letter of the second lot, thirty, divide this number in thirty-three parts. The same applies if the letter of the first lot is three, and the letter of the second lot, a hundred: divide in one hundred-three parts. So it is if the first letter is from the tens, like twenty, and the second hundreds, like two-hundreds. Divide them in two-hundred-twenty parts. This is the method for all letters. So is it if both letters are tens; you divide in ninety parts, and if they are hundreds, you divide in nine hundreds.

216

Do not worry; you will be soon saved from this trouble.	*Avk'ashk* (אוכעשף)
It will last a bit longer and then end.	*Bzlpttz* (בזלפתץ)
It will last longer but eventually cease.	*G'hmtzk* (גחמצך)
It is big and strong. You cannot take it; run away if you can.	*Dtnqs* (דטנקס)
You cannot run away from it; accept it with love.	*Hysrn* (היסרן)

217

Solitude is good for you, and you must be strong. Do not be afraid of what you see; you will soon attain what you asked for.

Solitude is good for you, but you will only attain it with great difficulty. You will not be answered right away; it will take time. But you must wait, for it will come.

You will only attain solitude through friends, for you cannot do it alone. It is too hard for you, and you will not be answered immediately.

If you want to go into solitude, you need watching and a trusting heart.

Do not go into solitude; you will not attain it, for you are faint-hearted, and you will get hurt.

218

If you want to know which day of the week is good for you to leave the city, put together the letter of the first lot with that of the second one, divide the result according to the seven days of the week. Wherever the count ends is the good day for you to go.

219

This newborn will be wise and wealthy.	*Ayq* (איק)
He will be wise, but not wealthy.	*Bkr* (בכר)
He will be wealthy, but not wise.	*Glsh* (גלש)
He will not be wise, neither stupid nor wealthy.	*Dmt* (דמת)
He will be average in wisdom and not wealthy.	*Hnk* (הנך)
He will be wise, but average in wealth.	*Vsm* (וסם)

He will be average in wisdom and in wealth.   *Z'an* (זען)

He will be wealthy and stupid.   *ḥpp* (חפף)

He will have neither wealth nor wisdom.   *Ṭtztz* (טצץ)

220

He who hits so and so is Jewish.   *A'hst* (אחסת)

It is an Arab.   *Bṭ'ak* (בטעך)

[99] It is a Gentile.   *Gypm* (גיפם)

It is a Jewish apostate.   *Dktzn* (דכצן)

It is a Gentile who became a Moslem.   *Hlqp* (הלקף)

It is a Gentile who became a proselyte.   *Vmrtz* (ומרץ)

It is a Moslem who became a Gentile.   *Znsh* (זנש)

221

You will profit this way.   *Avk'ashp* (אוכעשף)

You will not profit so much.   *Bzlpttz* (בזלפתץ)

You will lose money, but you will attain something better than money.   *G'hmtzk* (גחמצך)

Thieves will come and steal your money.   *Dṭnqs* (דטנקס)

There is danger for your life on this way.   *Hysrn* (היסרן)

222

This woman loves you much.   *Adzym'aqtn* (אדזימעקתן)

She neither loves nor hates you.	*Bh'hknprkp* (בההחכנפרדף)
She hates you.	*Gvṭlstzshstz* (גוטלסצשסץ)

223

If you want to know how many letters there are in the thief's name, see paragraph 121, and you will know how many letters there are in his name.

224

There are pirates at sea.	*Adzym'aq* (אדזימעק)
There are no pirates there yet, but they will come.	*Bh'hknprkp* (בההחכנפרדף)
There are no pirates there, for they went somewhere else.	*Gvṭlstzshm* (גוטלסצשסם)

[100]

225

The pirates are French.	*Amn* (אמן)
They are Chinese.	*Bnp* (בנף)
They are Maltese.	*Gstz* (גסץ)
They are Moroccan.	*Zr'a* (זאע)
They are English.	*Hp* (הפ)
They are Venetian.	*Vtz* (וצ)
They are Tripolitan.	*Zq* (זק)
They are Tunisian.	*'hr* (חר)

They are Algerian.	*Ṭsh* (טש)
They are renegades.	*Yt* (ית)
They are from Prague.	*Kk* (כך)
They are from Pisang [East].	*Lm* (לם)

226

This year the Arabs will be victorious.	*Aṭpn* (אטפן)
They will be victorious but have a great loss.	*Bytzp* (ביצף)
They will be victorious on the field but not in the fortresses.	*Qkptz* (קכקץ)
This year the Christians will be victorious.	*Dlr* (דלר)
They will be victorious but have a great loss.	*Ḥmsh* (המש)
They will be victorious on the field, but not in the fortresses.	*Vnt* (ונת)
Both sides will have great loss, and no one will be victorious.	*Zsk* (זסך)
They will prepare for war, but make peace between themselves.	*'h 'am* (חעם)

227

This store bears good luck for you.	*Aḥṭmpshn* (אהטמפשן)
The choice is yours.	*Bvyntztp* (בוינצתף)
[101] It is good for you, but thieves will scare you.	*Gzksqrtz* (גזכסקרץ)
Do not take it: it is not good for you.	*D'hl'arm* (דחלערם)

228

It is good to buy this maidservant.	*Ahtmpshn* (אהטמפשן)
She is good, but she will fornicate.	*Bvyntztp* (בוינצתף)
She is good, but she will run away.	*Gzksqktz* (גזכסקקדץ)
Do not buy her; she will die soon.	*D'hl'ars* (דחלעארס)

229

This object was stolen between sunset and nightfall.	*Ahtmpshn* (אהטמפשן)
It was stolen during the night.	*Bvyntztp* (בוינצתף)
It was stolen between dawn and sunrise.	*Gzksqktz* (גזכסקקדץ)
It was stolen during the day.	*D'hl'arm* (דחלערם)

230

The messenger will quickly come back.	*Ahtmpshn* (אהטמפשן)
He is late because he is making more money.	*Bvyntztp* (בוינצתף)
If he is ever found, he will come back, otherwise not.	*Gzksqktz* (גזכסקקדץ)
He does not want to come back.	*D'hl'arm* (דחלערם)

231

If you want to know how many sicknesses you will have in your lifetime, you must know that the twelve constellations have a beginning, a middle, and an end, which are thirty-six parts.

Therefore, put together both lots and divide the result according to thirty-six parts, and wherever the count ends is the number of sicknesses you will have in your lifetime.

[102]

232

No trespass was committed against this deposit.	*Aḥtmpshn* (אהטמפשן)
The guardian did not trespass but thought of it.	*Bvyntztp* (בוינצתף)
He did not trespass, but he is advised to do so.	*Gzksqktz* (גזכסקדץ)
Trespass was already done.	*D'hl'arm* (דחלערם)

233

He is honest and will not deny.	*Aḥtmpshn* (אהטמפשן)
He does not have it, but he will deny if you prosecute him.	*Bvyntztp* (בוינצתף)
If you want to prosecute this man, hide witnesses behind the fence to prevent his denial afterward.	*Gzksqktz* (גזכסקדץ)
Behave cautiously with him, for he will deny everything.	*D'hl'arm* (דחלערם)

234

If you want to know which day of the week to sit in the store, see paragraph 218.

235

If you want to know which day of the month to sit in the store, see paragraph 211.

236

If you want to know under which star to occupy the house, see paragraph 112.

237

If you want to know which day of the week to pass through the town, do what is said in paragraph 218.

[103]

238

If you want to know which day of the month to enter the city, see paragraph 211.

239

If you want to know which country is good for you, place all the countries you desire in front of you and add one. For instance, if there are twenty, arrange twenty-one parts. Wherever the count of the casting ends, is the country that is good for you. If it ends on twenty-one twice, know that you will not have any rest in these countries. Arrange other countries and divide them according to their number. Wherever the count ends is the country that is good for you.

240

So and so came to test you and speaks the truth. *Aḥtmpshn* (אהטמפשן)

He speaks the truth and does not test you. *Bvyntztp* (בוינצתף)

He did not come to test you; send him away without news. *Gzksqktz* (גזכסקדץ)

He came to test you. *D'hl'arm* (דחלערם)

241

This pregnant woman will not miscarry. *Aḥtmpshn* (אהטמפשן)

She has contractions, but she will not miscarry. *Bvyntztp* (בוינצתף)

Give her medicine, and she will not miscarry. *Gzksqktz* (גזכסקדץ)

She will miscarry; so it was decreed. *D'hl'arm* (דחלערם)

242

Your daughter-in-law gave birth to a boy. *Avk'ashp* (אוכעשף)

She is in labor and will soon deliver. *Bzlpttz* (בזלפתץ)

[104] Her time to deliver did not yet arrive. *G'hmtzk* (גחמצך)

She is in labor and it is hard; the child will not survive. *Dṭnqs* (דטנקס)

She is in labor and will not survive. *Hysrn* (היסרן)

243

Your wife gave birth and she is healthy.	*Azmqn* (אזמקן)
She had problems during delivery, and the baby died.	*B'hnrp* (בחנרף)
She is in labor and will be safe.	*Gtsshtz* (גטסשץ)
Her time to give birth has not arrived yet.	*Dy'at* (דיעת)
It was a false pregnancy.	*Hkpk* (הכפך)
She had a hard delivery and died.	*Vltzm* (ולצם)

244

You will soon find a lost object.	*Ahtmpshn* (אהטמפשן)
You will find a lost object at the end of your life.	*Bvyntztp* (בוינצתף)
You will have a son who will find it.	*Gzksqktz* (גזכסקדץ)
You will not find a lost object.	*D'hl'arm* (דחלערם)

245

You prayer was heard and your request accepted.	*Avk'ashp* (אוכעשף)
Only part of it was accepted.	*Bzlpttz* (בזלפתץ)
Your prayer was not accepted.	*G'hmtzk* (גחמצך)
Accusers did not leave it in peace.	*Dtnqs* (דטנקס)
Your prayer will not be accepted; the decree is irreversible.	*Hysrn* (היסרן)

246

Your will not be poor anymore; your luck is increasing.   *Azmqn* (אזמקן)

You will be neither poor nor rich, but will earn your living.   *B'hnrp* (בחנרף)

[105] You will father a son who will support you in your old age.   *Gtsshtz* (גטססשץ)

You will marry a woman whose star will bring you profit.   *Dy'at* (דיעת)

You will be poor until you leave this town.   *Hkpk* (הכפך)

You will be poor all the days of your life.   *Vltzm* (ולצם)

247

Reuven will die before Shimon.   *Avk'ashp* (אוכעשף)

Shimon will die before Reuven.   *Bzlpttz* (בזלפתץ)

Reuven will die thirty days before Shimon.   *G'hmtzk* (גחמצך)

Shimon will die thirty days before Reuven.   *Dtnqs* (דטנקס)

They will both die the same day.   *Hysrn* (היסרן)

248

Your deeds are agreeable to God and to people.   *Avk'ashp* (אוכעשף)

They are agreeable to God, but not very much to people.   *Bzlpttz* (בזלפתץ)

They are agreeable to God but not at all   *G'hmtzk* (גחמצך)

to people.

They are agreeable to people but not to God, for you act with haughtiness.   *Dtnqs* (דטנקס)

They are agreeable neither to God nor to people.   *Hysrn* (היסרן)

249

The messenger who went for the sake of the community does not have to stand before the ruler, his plea has already been granted.   *Ahtmpshn* (אהטמפשן)

He must go and will succeed with no trouble.   *Bvyntztp* (בוינצתף)

He will succeed but with great trouble.   *Gzksqktz* (גזכסקדץ)

He will not find grace by the ruler who will tie him in chains.   *D'hl'arm* (דחלערם)

[106]

250

If you want to know the place where your prayer went, cast the lot with perfect intention and divide the result in twenty-seven parts as follows: 1) Empty space, 2) Kingdom of the Material World, 3) Microprosopus of the Material World, 4) Mother of the Material World, 5) Father of the Material World, 6) Macroprosopus of the Material World, 7) Kingdom of Formation, 8) Microprosopus of Formation, 9) Mother of Formation, 10) Father of Formation, 11) Macroprosopus of Formation, 12) Kingdom of Creation, 13) Microprosopus of Creation, 14) Mother of Creation, 15) Father of Creation, 16) Macroprosopus of Creation, 17) Rachel of the Divine World, 18) Jacob of the Divine World, 19) Leah of the Divine World, 20) Israel the Lad (*Na'ar*) of the Divine World, 21) Understanding of the Divine World, 22) Israel of the Divine World, 23) Mother of the Divine World, 24) Father of the Divine World,

25) Macroprosopus of the Divine World, 26) Holy Ancient One (*Atiqa Qadisha*), 27) Ancient of Days (*Atiq Yomin*).

If the count ends in the first part, which is empty, know that your prayer did not go anywhere. If it ended anywhere else, it is the place reached by your prayer.

251

If you want to know which worlds were unified by you, arrange the reunifications (*ha-Ye'hudim*) as follows: 1) Foundation and Kingdom of the Material World, 2) Victory and Glory of the Material World, 3) Wisdom and Severity of the Material World, 4) Wisdom and Understanding of the material World, 5) Face to face reflection (*Histakluth Anpin be-Anpin*) of Crown in Beauty of the Material World, 6) Foundation and Kingdom of the Material World, 7) Victory and Glory of Formation, 8) Wisdom and Severity of Formation, 9) Wisdom and Understanding of Formation, 10) Face to face reflection of Crown in Beauty of Formation, 11) Foundation and Kingdom of Creation, 12) Victory and Glory of Creation, 13) Wisdom and Severity of Creation, 14) Wisdom and Understanding of Creation, 15) Face to face reflection of Crown in Beauty of Creation, 16) Jacob and Rachel of the Divine World, 17) Yeshurun and Leah of the Divine World, 18) Israel the Patriarch (*Israel Saba*) and Beauty of the Divine World, 19) Father and Mother of the Divine World, 20) Face to face reflection of Macroprosopus in Microprosopus of the Divine World [107], 21) Three ties of Faithfulness in perfect reunification (*Tlath Qishre de-Meheimnuta be-Ye'huda Shlim*). After arranging these twenty-one levels, divide the lots in twenty-one parts, and wherever the count ends, from there and below the worlds were reunited.

252

If you want to know how many letters there are in the name of the Messiah, follow the instructions of paragraph 121 concerning reincarnation, and you shall be able to derive the name of the last savior.

253

If you want to know how old the Messiah son of David is, cast a lot as mentioned, divide it in one-hundred-twenty years. Wherever the count ends is his age.

254

The Messiah will come in your days and redeem Israel.   *Ahṭmpshn* (אהטממפשן)

You will merit to see the Messiah, the ingathering of exiles, and the rebuilding of the temple.   *Bvyntztp* (בוינצתף)

The Messiah will come right after you die.   *Gzksqktz* (גזכסקקדץ)

The Messiah will come in the days of your children.   *D'hl'arm* (דחלערם)

255

If you want to know in which direction, or in which corner of the world the Messiah is located, arrange eight parts as follows: 1) east, 2) south, 3) west, 4) north, 5) southeast corner, 6) southwest corner, 7) northwest corner, 8) northeast corner. Wherever the count of the lot ends is the direction or the corner. Once [108] you know the direction, arrange the cities of that part of the world, and wherever the count of the lot ends is the city where the Messiah lives. If you want an alternative way, arrange all countries of the world, and wherever the count ends, he lives. Once you know the country, arrange all its cities, and wherever the count of the lot ends is the city where he lives. There you shall seek and find him.

256

If you want to know in which year the redemption of Israel will be, arrange the years, from the time you live until the end of the sixth millennium, which is 5999. Divide the number of the lot according to the number lying in front of you, and wherever the count ends is the year where our king, the Messiah of God, will come, rebuild the temple, and bring back the exiles. May it be soon, and so may it be His will. Amen, amen, and may the Almighty do so.

So ends the Book of Oracles

composed by the godly Rabbi Chaim Vital

of blessed memory.

Praise to the revered One!

Other volumes in the series:

Sheva Netivot Ha-Torah – The Seven Paths of Torah
by Avraham Abulafia
Integral edition in English and Hebrew

This book demonstrates the primacy of Kabbalah over every other branch of knowledge. It classifies seven levels of understanding of the Torah, showing what they are and how to reach them.

Or Ha-Sechel - Light of the Mind
by Avraham Abulafia
Integral edition in English and Hebrew

This book was written by Abulafia as a personal instruction for one of his disciples, learned in philosophy. By combining philosophy and kabbalah, the author uncovers in a logical way and by examples the keys and the techniques of Kabbalah. Thus, the access to the higher worlds is disclosed in a natural fashion.

Chaye Ha-Olam Ha-Ba – Life in the World to Come
by Avraham Abulafia
Integral edition in English and Hebrew

This major text by Abulafia concerns Prophetic Kabbalah. It is essentially a "book of names", of advanced Kabbalah. It is not written for beginners, but rather for those who are already on the path. There are not many explanations; the only important thing is the combinations of names to employ in meditation in order to open the holy gates and to reach the state of the restored Adam. Upon his return to Paradise, one can enjoy its fruits while still live physically on earth. The book investigates expecially the 72 Names of God.

Sefer Ha-Ot – The Book of the Sign
by Avraham Abulafia
Integral edition in English and Hebrew

This is one of the rare autobiographic books in Kabbalah. Abulafia relates his experiences and visions, some of which are really frightening. Most notable are his encounters with angels.

Other volumes in the series:

Sulam Aliyah – Ladder of Ascent
by Yehudah Albotini
Integral edition in English and Hebrew

This book explains in a very detailed manner the most secret kabbalistic techniques for attaining enlightenment and access to the higher realms of consciousness. Albotini summarizes very clearly the Abulafian system, while disclosing the paths for the sincere researchers. Thus, the gates of heaven will be open, making it possible to once again eat of the fruits of the Tree of Life.

Shaarei Kedusha – Gates of Holiness
by Chaim Vital
Integral edition in English, Hebrew and Aramaic

This text of prophetic Kabbalah teaches how to create the "external" and "internal" environment for successfully receiving the "Spirit of Propechy". It presents a clear, precise and revolutionary method for the one who feels the call but has gotten lost along the way and failed to reach the state of enlightenment.

Shaarei Tzedek - Gates of Justice
by Rabbi Shem Tov Sefardi of Leon
Integral edition in English

As Moshe Idel demonstrated, this book is incorrectly attributed to Rabbi Shem Tov Sefardi de Leon. Its apparently true author is a direct disciple of Avraham Abulafia, Natan ben Saadyah Harar. He describes instructions he received from his teacher, believed to be Aubulafia himself, along with his ecstatic experiences. This gives the book unparalleled importance, as auto-biographical works in Kabbalah are extremely rare. Additionally, he explains in detail many kabbalistic techniques, the very ones he employed to reach his prophetical states. The full text is a reconstruction based upon the four original known manuscripts, which in general have some notable differences or omissions.

Providence University:

Our University is affiliated to ULC (Universal Life Church), and operates in conjunction with the congregation ULC-ITALIA, an inter-faith and non-denominational church.

We sponsor the translation and promote the diffusion of kabbalistic texts, with particular attention to the teachings of Prophetic Kabbalah, while at the same time divulging the ways that permit a direct experience of God.

Most of our translations are of fundamental and often cited ancient Hebrew and Aramaic texts that have never before translated into English or any other language.

We do this, "for the earth shall be full of the knowledge of the Lord, as the waters cover the sea" (Isaiah 11:9). "And they shall teach no more every man his neighbor, and every man his brother, saying, Know the Lord: for they shall all know me, from the least of them unto the greatest of them". (Jeremiah 31:34)

Courses and lectures:

Providence University is persistently engaged in organizing courses, lectures, and seminars. We operate in many countries.

At our website, http://www.everburninglight.org/, you will find more information about our activities and agenda.

You may contact us by E-mail at info@everburninglight.org

If you cannot physically partecipate in our meetings, you may join us by videoconference; we have weekly meetings. If you have internet access, you can partecipate. Write us and we will send you further instructions.

For snail mail, we answer only if you contact us through our joint congregation in Italy. The address is:
ULC-ITALIA
via C.A. Colombo 20/F
34074 Monfalcone (GO)
ITALY

For urgent communications, you can contact our joint congregation in Italy at the following number:
+39-347-2295140